Mirrors *of* Transformation

The Philadelphia Association of Jungian Analysts

THE PHILADELPHIA ASSOCIATION OF JUNGIAN ANALYSTS, INC. (PAJA) was founded in 1984 for the purposes of professional and public education in the theory and practice of analytical psychology. In 1994, PAJA founded the C. G. Jung Institute of Philadelphia for the purpose of advanced Jungian education and training for professionals and other serious students of Jungian thought.

ADDRESS INQUIRIES TO
PAJA
c/o Dr. James Hollis
1023 Oak Avenue
Linwood, NJ 08221

Also by PAJA

Dreams, Dreamers and Dreaming. Papers by Alexander McCurdy III, Jole Cappiello McCurdy, Polly Young-Eisendrath, James Hollis, Seth Isaiah Rubin, Stephen Martin.

The Architecture of the Soul: The Use of Myth and Fairy Tale in Depth Psychology. Papers by Stephen Martin, David Hart, Polly Young-Eisendrath, Alexander McCurdy III, Alden Josey, James Hollis.

ADDRESS INQUIRIES ABOUT THESE PUBLICATIONS TO
The Round Table Press
P.O. Box 475
Southeastern, PA 19399

Mirrors *of* Transformation

The Self in Relationships

THE PAJA PAPERS

Essays by Jungian Analysts

Marita Digney
James Hollis
Alden Josey
Stephen Martin
Alexander McCurdy III
Polly Young-Eisendrath

Edited by
Dolores Elise Brien

The Round Table Press
Berwyn, Pennsylvania
1995

The Round Table Press

P.O. Box 475
Southeastern, PA 19399

261 Dayleview Road
Berwyn, PA 19312

Mirrors of Transformation:
The Self in Relationships

The essays in *Mirrors of Transformation: The Self in Relationships* were originally presented as papers at symposia sponsored by the Philadelphia Association of Jungian Analysts on November 2, 1991, and October 10, 1993, and at the C. G. Jung Commemorative Lecture, sponsored by the C. G. Jung Foundation of the Delaware Valley, June 6, 1993.

Cover photo courtesy of the Print and Picture Collection of the Free Library of Philadelphia.

PRINTED IN THE UNITED STATES OF AMERICA

LIBRARY OF CONGRESS CATALOGING-IN-PUBLICATION DATA

Mirrors of transformation : the self in relationships : essays / by Jungian analysts Marita Digney . . . [et al.] ; edited by Dolores Elise Brien.
p. cm. -- (THE PAJA PAPERS)
ISBN 1-882275-06-3
1. INDIVIDUATION (PSYCHOLOGY) 2. JUNG, C. G. (CARL GUSTAV), 1875-1961. 3. INTERPERSONAL RELATIONS. I. DIGNEY, MARITA. II. BRIEN, DOLORES ELISE. III. SERIES.
BF175.5 I53M57 1995
155.2'5--DC20 94-49053
CIP

The Self is relatedness; the Self doesn't exist without relationship. Only when the Self mirrors itself in so many mirrors does it really exist. . . . You can never come to your Self by building a meditation hut on top of Mount Everest; you will only be visited by your own ghosts and that is not individuation. . . You are all alone with yourself and the Self doesn't exist. . . . Not that you are, but that you do is the Self. The Self appears in your deeds, and deeds always mean relationship.

C. G. Jung
Seminar on Nietzsche's *Zarathustra*
(1934-1939). Part 6, Lecture 2

Contents

Mirrors *of* Transformation

Editor's Note

CW refers throughout to the *Collected Works of C. G. Jung* (Princeton, N.J.: Princeton University Press).

Burn In Water, Wash in Fire: Paradox and Ambiguity in the Work of Individuation

Alden Josey

> [It is vital] for a paradox to be accepted and tolerated and respected, and for it not to be resolved. By flight to split-off intellectual functioning, it is possible to resolve the paradox, but the price of this is the loss of the value of the paradox itself.
>
> D. W. Winnicott, *Playing and Reality,* xii

In a brief essay that introduced his epoch-making work, *Symbols of Transformation*, Jung called attention to two kinds of thinking: directed thinking, which operates with logical and rational elements to build up structures "for the purpose of communication, and is difficult and exhausting"; and dreaming or fantasy-thinking, which is effortless, works spontaneously with the contents ready at hand and is "guided by unconscious motives." In making this distinction, he called attention to the possibility of prizing one kind of thinking over the other to such an extent that our lives become trapped in a limiting psychic one-sidedness. Naturally, what is rejected by consciousness falls into the unconscious where it acts autonomously as a split-off and subversive shadow content.

But, inevitably, we will find the psyche attempting to set the balance right. Especially in the all-too-common tendency to overvalue conscious, directed thinking, it presents us with a vast range of symbolic imagery and paradoxical forms that baffle and defeat our mere logic in order to offer something of the deeper and more beautiful truth of the creative unconscious.

Tertullian, a father of the Christian Church (155-225 A.D.), said: "And the Son of God is dead, which is worthy of belief because it is absurd. And when buried He rose again, which is certain because it is impossible." The shocking contradiction of these statements is both fascinating and repellent. Fascinating because they seem to be hiding in their stark antinomies some mysterious and compelling wisdom. Repellent because they disturb our sense of the orderly and logical structure of language and of the inner cosmos of ideas, meanings and values.

In "Revelations of Divine Love," recorded in 1373, Dame Julian of Norwich, a remarkable woman of great simplicity and spiritual depth, wrote: "In a revelation, God showed me a tiny thing, no bigger than a hazelnut, lying in the palm of the hand, and as round as a ball. I looked at it, puzzled, and thought 'What is it?' The answer came: 'It is everything that is made.' I wondered how it could survive. It was so small that I expected it to shrivel up and disappear. Then I was answered, 'It exists now and always because God loves it.' Thus I understood that everything exists through the love of God." It is worth recalling in this context the recent announcements of astronomers' discoveries that support the Big Bang theory of cosmic origins and suggest that all matter in the universe was originally confined in a space much smaller than the size of an atom.

The reader may, at this point, be thinking that he or she is being offered a sermon, one narrowly drawn to some aspects of a Christian viewpoint, rather than a discussion of psychological matters. I assure you this is not so, but simply a reflection of the fact that before there was a differentiated perception of the psychological meaning of human experience, psychic reality was often expressed in the language of religious or philosophical discourse. The corollary is that it is absolutely vital that we read inherited religious literature with a psychological understanding in order to appreciate the universal and archetypal nature of its truths. With this attitude, one can recognize that, for example, Dame Julian's paradoxical revelation is an aspect of a woman's individuation process long before there were any psychologists around to describe it as such.

In 1924, Carl Gustav Jung said: "Nearly every psychological principle, every truth relating to the psyche, must, if it is to be made absolutely true, immediately be reversed." And, in another place, he added: "The only statements that have psychological validity concerning the God-image are either paradoxes or antinomies" (CW12, par. 11 n6). "A religion becomes inwardly impoverished when it loses or waters down its paradoxes; but their multiplication enriches because only the paradox comes anywhere near to comprehending the fulness of life. Non-ambiguity and non-contradiction are one-sided and thus unsuited to express the incomprehensible" (CW12, par. 18). In other words, if we open ourselves to the reality of the psyche, it will require that we endure the tension of contradictory truths.

Finally, in his essay "Principles of Practical Psychotherapy" in 1935, he wrote: "A great number of antinomies is required to describe the nature of the psyche satisfactorily. One of the fundamental antinomies is the statement that psyche depends on body and body depends on psyche. There are clear proofs for both sides of this antinomy, so that an objective judgment cannot give more weight to thesis or to antithesis. The existence of valid contradictions shows that the object of investigation presents the inquiring mind with exceptional difficulties, as a result of which only relatively valid statements can be made, at least for the time being" (CW16, par. 1).

Thus we have it that these very different individuals, speaking over a span of 1700 years, one as interpreter and defender of a faith, another as a reclusive mystic, and the last as a medical psychologist, draw our attention to the inadequacies of language and syntax, the products of a differentiating and discursive intellect, to describe the paradoxical nature of the psyche and its deepest processes. In Jung's concept of the Self, at once the central organizing principle and the psychic totality, we find the sharp scent of paradox right at the center of his model of the psyche.

We are bound by experience to acknowledge that there are truths and realities that present themselves to us, which cannot be comprehended within the logical-causal structures of ego consciousness. This machinery of thought and expression is simply not adequate and, at its best, points the way beyond itself to the inexpressible. This is, of course, the meaning and function of the symbol, and the cultivation of a symbolic attitude toward life is central to the work of individuation, the process of successive approximations to a unity of one's scattered selves.

One of the indispensable qualities of a Jungian perspective on the psyche is the awareness of the tension, a profoundly creative tension, that this situation puts into our ordinary conscious experience. I want to emphasize the principle that a deep-reaching psychic healing experience requires the brave and active pursuit of ambiguity and tolerance of its tensions. The task of the analyst/therapist is to bring into the analytic space not the illusion of peace, but a sword, not the easing of internal tensions per se, but their suffering and transformation into new conscious standpoints.

As thinking animals in the object-filled maze of everyday living, we urgently need clear, straightforward expressions of solid, demonstrable truth. We are anxious and resistant when truth appears in ambiguous and paradoxical form. Sometimes we are merely puzzled; sometimes we are violently antagonistic. It is not difficult to see these reactions as variations of a defense employed by the ego against the unknown abyss of the unconscious.

This is as true of the analyst/therapist as it is for the analysand/patient. The therapeutic community gains a great comfort, I suspect, and a useful defense against the chaotic-seeming nature of the unconscious from its nosological classification of mental disorder. The *Diagnostic and Statistical Manual of Mental Disorders* of the American Psychiatric Association is useful in bringing together some thinking about the psyche and its vicissitudes, but it seems to me, in another way, to be a potentially deceptive document, with its implication that the diagnostic distinctions it makes—necessarily statistical in their weight—may be applied without qualification to the personal situation of a specific individual.

I was astonished to find William Blake quoted in a recent issue of the scientific journal *Nature* to this very point: "He who would do good to another must do it in Minute Particulars. General Good is the plea of the scoundrel, hypocrite and flatterer; for Art and Science cannot exist but in minutely organized Particulars." Minutely organized Particulars! What a wonderful phrase to describe the painstaking and sometimes painful therapeutic process of individuation.

With respect to the neuroses, for example, the more our knowledge gains in differentiated theoretical and clinical detail, the more massively collective and statistical it becomes, the less it expresses the most important things about the nature of the illness of a particular person with a particular history. Or, as Jung said, "It is totally irrelevant." Jung commented on this paradoxical situation by offering another one: "A second fundamental antinomy in psychology runs: the individual signifies nothing in comparison with the universal, and the universal signifies nothing in comparison with the individual. There are, as we all know, no universal elephants, only individual elephants." Here is an "organized Particular" that is not so minute!

In his development of analytical psychology from his early clinical and psycho-cultural studies as well as from his relationship with Freud, Jung saw clearly the limitations of a late-nineteenth-century scientific materialism in constructing a model of the psyche that fully comprehended the nonrational, symbolic nature of its unconscious, archetypal ground. This earned him in due time the scorn of the "scientists" of psychology. Yet, he was, in fact, more scientific than his critics because he was willing to include a wider and richer field of experimental observation than they. In this, he was squarely in the stream of the revolutionary development of

Western thought and *Weltanschauung* that has taken place within the twentieth century.

Jung's psychology as it developed in the first three decades of this century mirrored in a fascinating way the unfolding drama of scientific perception of natural reality, particularly concerning the profound paradoxes in the physical structure of the world. The classical Newtonian world was in shock as the new quantum theory began to turn the world upside down. Let us see how some of these developments relate to parallel events in the development of analytical psychology.

In 1897, exactly fifty years before I began the serious study of chemistry, J. J. Thomson, a British physicist, discovered the electron. It is startling to realize that at this very recent date, the existence of atoms had not been conclusively proved, for there had been neither the theory nor an effective experimental approach to this level of the physical world.

In 1905, Einstein's work on Brownian motion settled the issue of the physical reality of molecules, and his special theory of relativity introduced the mind-shaking idea that in the microcosmic world, objects had the dual nature of particles and of waves. Here we see a disturbing paradox forcing its way into perceptions of the physical world. In one author's words: "Many physicists considered [these ideas] absurd." When Niels Bohr announced in 1910 a theory of atomic structure containing radical new notions about what electrons are and how they behave, two prominent German physicists (Stern and von Laue) swore to give up physics if he was correct. As Bohr's ideas were confirmed, they recanted and later made significant contributions to the emerging new physics.

Recall that Freud's *Interpretation of Dreams* appeared in

1900, and by 1907 Jung had published the first of his *Psychiatric Studies* and his early *Experimental Researches,* including work on the association test and its fruit, the theory of complexes. He also was beginning to find ways to investigate a hidden and inaccessible world, the unconscious psyche. Jung's research showed the relativization of time and space in the unconscious where old experience organized in the form of affectively toned complexes still retained the power to determine responses and even to dominate life in the field of ego consciousness.

In 1924, a young French graduate student, Prince Louis de Broglie, suggested that Thomson's electron, still widely considered a particle, could also be described as having wave nature. The hoots of derision were loud, and one physicist suggested the idea be called "la Comédie Française." I mention this to point out with what contempt and fear the old order greeted the paradoxical character of the new theories which, nevertheless, were being confirmed by experiment.

Not long after, in 1925-1926, Erwin Schrödinger and Werner Heisenberg independently advanced theories that coalesced to form the new quantum mechanics, a radical treatment of the nature of physical reality that replaced all the old deterministic ideas of the world with the notion of probability. Suddenly, firm statements about the properties of the microcosmic world were no longer possible; velocity, location—all was indeterminate, hedged in probabilities.

It is hard to overstate the scope and depth of this revolution in thought about the nature of reality. At about the same time, in 1916, Jung published an essay titled "The Structure of the Unconscious," in which he wrote: "If, through assimilation of the unconscious, we make the mistake of including the collective psyche in the inventory of personal mental functions, a dissolution of the personality into its paired opposites inevitably follows . . . . How much these paired opposites are contained in the collective psyche is exemplified by primitives: one observer will extol the greatest virtues in them, while another will record the very worst impressions of the selfsame tribe. For the primitive, whose personal differentiation is, as we know, only just beginning, both judgments are true, because his mentality is essentially collective" (CW 7, par. 458).

In commenting on his deepening insight into the antinomies of the unconscious and its echoes in the new physics, Jung wrote in 1935: "Thus we are faced in psychotherapy with a situation comparable with that in modern physics where, for instance, there are two contradictory theories of light . . . Contradictions in a department of science merely indicate that its subject displays characteristics which at present can be grasped only by means of antinomies—witness the wave theory and the corpuscular theory of light."

As physicists continue to the present to overthrow the old deterministic ideas about nature, more astonishing and disconcerting notions are discussed and, where possible, subjected to experimental testing. For example, in the November 1991 issue of the popular journal *Scientific American* there is a serious discussion of the idea that all physical phenomena—from the vanishingly small to the incomprehensibly huge—arise from so-called "superstrings . . . wriggling in no fewer than ten dimensions"! And, in the "many-worlds" interpretation of quantum mechanics, every time an atom decays, huge, possibly infinite, numbers of duplicates of the universe, including our own physical selves, are created. This fantastic theoretical notion has the flavor of the purest science fiction, but serious physicists have found no way to disprove it.

The point of this excursion into the history of modern physics is to show how thoroughly ideas of paradox and ambiguity have penetrated into contemporary conceptions of "the way things are," even in this most rational and logical aspect of mental life. We have all been deprived of the illusory comfort of living in a world of clear-cut choices and unambiguous alternatives from which undesired conflicts and complications have been excluded. The discoveries of Jung make it clear how much the psyche, beyond the narrow band of ego consciousness, is fundamentally rooted in contradiction, paradox and ambiguity. Now we have to look more closely into the meaning of these ideas as they come into personal life and are manifested in our own personal work of individuation.

The goal of the individuation process is the transformation of consciousness both in the scope and depth of its contents and in its relationship with the unconscious psyche. In order for ego consciousness to achieve a new dimension, the ego must continually yield its position in what seems to be, what is often experienced as, an act of agonizing self-sacrifice. Here we see at once the paradoxical nature of this process and why it is the source of so much conflict. The old, inadequate structures of a life are confronted with radically transforming new images and energies that feel to ego consciousness like nothing less than its death. This is an inner, psychological process of development that is imaged in Christian and pre-Christian myth as the death and resurrection of a god figure.

In Plato's *Phaedo*, Socrates says: "It is a fact, Simmias,

that true philosophers make dying their profession, and that to them of all men death is least alarming." Jung wrote that "the experience of the self is always a defeat for the ego" (CW14, par. 788). I think these two insights speak of the same psychic reality. They recognize the psychological truth, reminiscent of the alchemists' *mortificatio*, that enlarging the limits of consciousness through an encounter with the unconscious may constellate the emotional experience of a kind of crucifixion, as noted above. This death is tolerated (died, as it were) for the sake of the new life that it brings. In the involuntary *mortificatio*, not to say *solutio*, of a psychotic episode, very often there are vivid images of actual or impending death.

The ego, from the earliest phase of its development, necessarily attempts to create stable situations in a world of objects (inner and outer) characterized by the dualities of the opposites. This is an adaptive response to life with its antinomies of good and evil, light and dark, pain and pleasure, and it secures the individual's existence in the world against internal and external forces that might threaten it. Thus, the ego is "now-" or even "past-oriented," as it must be in its function of selecting and judging, while the Self presses for an unfolding manifestation and is significantly "prospective" or "future-oriented." "Everything psychic," Jung wrote in *Mysterium Coniunctionis*, "is pregnant with the future." Ego consciousness, as the agent of "directed process" and of the "now," is constantly in danger of running into one-sidedness if it is isolated from the balancing compensations of the unconscious.

This conflict between the goals of the ego and the goals of the Self is a kind of "thesis-antithesis," the contest of two seemingly irreconcilable standpoints, and its resolution, which is never final or complete, seems to be the synthesis of ever more comprehensive consciousness as successive "theses" generate successive "antitheses" and higher and higher syntheses in new states of awareness. This dialectic within the psyche is of central importance to the Jungian perspective on psychic life, leading the American Jungian analyst Edward Edinger to declare that "the purpose of life is the creation of consciousness."

The one-sidedness that develops through overvaluation of the conscious standpoint leads inexorably to the buildup of an energized, compensatory position in the unconscious that is discharged in various ways from, say, normal dreaming to psychosis.

On the other hand, by recognizing that the development of consciousness is what the psyche is striving toward in the work of individuation, we can avoid the trap of overvaluing the unconscious. This is a trap many fall into, especially in their first exposure to Jungian ideas. It is a too easy substitution for the demanding and, in the alchemical sense, "mortifying" work of coming to terms with the contents of the unconscious. It overlooks the fact that within the vast treasure house of the unconscious, there is dross among the gold. The ego needs the unconscious for its enrichment and enlargement; it is also true that the unconscious needs the ego in order to become manifest in conscious life. This means that psychological wellness requires not only the development, or enlargement, of the conscious personality but also its relatedness to the unconscious psyche. This state of integration and balance is described as one with a strong and healthy ego-Self axis.

The dialectic between the adaptive ego consciousness and the compensating unconscious is what Jung called the "transcendent function." He wrote: "The confrontation of the two positions generates a tension charged with energy and creates a living, third thing . . . a movement out of the suspension between opposites, a living birth that leads to a new level of being, a new situation. The transcendent function manifests itself as a quality of conjoined opposites" (CW 8, par. 189). In the healing space of analytic psychotherapy, nothing is more important for either the analyst or the analysand than the process through which this "new level of being, a new situation" can be encountered.

In the analytic process, we often find the theme of paradox and ambiguity played out in dreams as the psyche tries to confront the ego with images that relativize and destabilize its one-sided position. For example, a woman had a dream in which a voice said, "The criminal makes the best therapist." This reference to the paradoxical healing power of the inferior and outcast aspect of psyche—the shadow—was very appropriate in this case in which a "false self," defended by a powerful thinking function, had become congealed around the woman's personality. Before the healing could begin, both the patient and the analyst needed to find a way to allow the suffering, hatred and existential fear associated with the "true self" to be experienced safely. Following the dream, this process took on a new momentum as both analyst and analysand opened themselves to the dark healing principle that it foreshadowed.

Let me relate another story of paradox and ambiguity, which is about a middle-aged European man who as a young teenager had an intense experience of what I call the childhood Self. This event occurred in a religious context so powerful that he remembered it as a conversion experience, a salvific moment when he felt contained and accepted by a reality greater than himself which he, of course, called God. As a result, the young man entered a Bible college in order to become a foreign missionary in his denomination. Having accomplished this goal, he became something of a "star," admired by all his colleagues. His intense inner experience had propelled him on a course of action which concretized his vision within sharply defined sectarian religious limits.

Not long after taking up his pastoral duties in a foreign country, he would preach to his congregation on Sundays and then travel to a distant town where another religious teacher held forth. During these religious meetings, he was critical of and even antagonistic toward the very ideas and doctrines that he espoused so well in his own church. His intelligence, verbal and thinking skills made him a virtual devil's advocate, an experience he found deeply gratifying. He told me about this remarkable split within himself with a mixture of amazement, chagrin and even a bit of humor at the paradox which his life had become.

As his story unfolded, it became obvious that, while he was preparing for a future role as a religious leader in his church, a counter position had developed in his psyche which attacked this young man's literal enactment of his epiphany of the Self. This internal opposition was defeated temporarily, however, by his strong sense of Christian duty and his feelings of guilt at its energies and images, often of an intensely erotic nature. Later, when he found that he could no longer believe and teach the dogmatic religious ideas that he had inherited in his church, he left the ministry and sought another profession.

When I met him, he was significantly depressed and

bereft of a sense of flow and movement in his life. Although he was extremely bright, verbal and creative, he did not feel that he was "living his life" and he did not know how to discover it.

He presented a dream in which he entered his library and, with a sense of exhilaration, sat down ready to work. But then he discovered that all his books on Western philosophy and literature were missing. Only the books on religion, mysticism and Eastern philosophy remained. A "numb helplessness" having set in, the dreamer awakened himself with a frightened cry of "Help!" We can see in this dream an image of a powerful antinomy, the paradoxical opposites of rationality and irrationality, along with a compensating shift toward the latter in the unconscious.

He had another dream in which he had handed an assigned paper to an instructor who began to inspect it but had, paradoxically, already critiqued and graded it. Here was an inner critic who acted in an a priori way, which for the dreamer carried the aura of arbitrariness and the authority to convict him of "Original Sin"! The dreamer argued about the grade with limited success and then left with the "encompassing sense that something fundamental to the way people live and think is about to change."

Later, the dreamer looks out into the streets upon an amazing and paradoxical scene—snow in July! As the dream ends, a group of black men start to dance, saying, "This calls for a celebration!" The dreamer is prevented from entering his office building by a "cackling court jester" whose costume is too big for the door.

In an earlier dream, one of great complexity and numinosity, the dreamer hears the voice of God saying "You must obey me." He then receives instructions to walk along the edge of a sunlit path, just off the path to the left and not on the path itself. He walks in the shadows a step or two away from the light. This reminded me of a Navajo myth describing the search of twin brothers for their father, the Sun. In their quest, the brothers meet with an ancient woman called Old Age, who gives them the same advice as the dreamer received: they are not to walk in her path but to the left side of it in order not to grow old, i.e., not to fall into the realm of space/time with its limitations. "Old age is on the right hand side," the story tells, "youth on the left." The dreamer had no knowledge of this story.

As the dream ends, the dreamer is brought by God into a semi-darkened cave and made to take part in a ritual during which animal skins are cast into a deep pit that already contains the decaying remains of other skins previously thrown there. The dreamer protests against the waste of useful skins; they could have been used instead as garments. Then God tells him, "Yes, it would have been better—but then you would not have learned how to do the irrational thing!" By "irrational thing" the dreamer understood that God meant him to "obey" him (God).

These dreams are rich in paradox. They have the force of an inner need on the part of the dreamer to rid himself of old tyrannies of thinking in the world of either/or, the world of the phenomenal pairs of opposites. The original experience of the childhood Self in the form of religious conversion was concretized into a specific decision and confined to a specific manifestation of it in the dogma of an established religious sect. This "conversion" released into his life an affirming flood of psychic energy and youthful vitality which was immediately divided between the natural and instinctive expressions, which had to be repressed, and a rational, belief-oriented religious view, with which he at once allied himself.

The repressed parts of the psyche asserted themselves in a shadow life in the seminary which caused considerable confusion and guilt. In retrospect, however, this "errant" behavior was probably an effort by the psyche to repair a dangerous split. As Jung affirmed,"the symptomatology of an illness is at the same time a natural attempt at healing" (CW 8, par. 312).

In the *enantiodromia* that occurred a few years later, the religious domain was eclipsed, and he apparently lost contact with it. Now there is a possibility of a new standpoint, one that can contain opposites more consciously, can feel the possibility that the inevitable loss of life that results from the ego/shadow split can be retrieved.

The effect of the paradox, whether in word or image, whether in the antinomies of the philosophers or in the grotesqueries of alchemy or of the dream, is to confound the rational mind, to bring to a halt all our discursive intellectuality and to open the way to a subjective experience of the Self. Within the analytic framework, "pregnant with the future," it is the obligation of the analyst or therapist to play midwife to that which gropes toward birth and, above all, not to cooperate with the resistance to contradictions or to the dissolution of the creative tension through which new states approach.

Lastly, we need to avoid the illusion, which I find un-Jungian, that individuation is an achievable goal. This is a trap laid by the unremitting quest of ego consciousness for a final state, an all-encompassing answer that dissolves life's confusions and ambiguities. Rather, it seems to me more tolerable and more human to believe that we can truly lay down the immense burden of having to "become individuated" and simply open ourselves more and more consciously to the mysterious beauty, the beautiful mystery of psyche.

Gender and Individuation: Relating to Self and Other

POLLY YOUNG-EISENDRATH

Before I can share with you my ideas regarding the role of gender in individuation, I want to introduce my perspective on these concepts. Both "gender" and "individuation" are under dispute among depth psychologists, and I want to clarify my view of the central issues. This clarification forms a major part of my presentation. It leads directly into an account of the clinical and theoretical implications of sex and gender differences and the process of individuation in adulthood.

We can no longer speak blithely of "the individuation of the self," or of a unified Self that unfolds from within, and expect to be readily received by many of our colleagues in depth psychology, theology, and philosophy. Theorists from many disciplines seriously question the usefulness of models of the self that assume that a bounded, individual self is universal. Some of our colleagues question *any* basic claim that the configuration or experience of self has a universal nature.

In a recent, generally supportive, review (Seidenberg 1991) of *Female Authority: Empowering Women Through Psy-*

chotherapy, a book I wrote with Florence Wiedemann, the psychiatrist reviewer was very critical of our use of Jung's psychology to defend our model of female development. He described analytical psychology as "steeped . . . in phylogenetic, mystical authoritarianism" (p. 227). Although I disagree with some of his critique (e.g., that Jungians invent dream interpretations to fit their own concepts), I am sympathetic to many of his remarks.

Like the reviewer, I am opposed to a form of realism that can creep into analytical psychology. It is a belief that the "really real" lies beyond experience. It is a way of speaking that seems to indicate that we can step outside of our own context and read pristine signs of universality in everyday events, like dreams. Pronouncements about "the collective unconscious" or the Self can sound as though one has a "god's eye view" of human affairs. Jung sometimes speaks as though he "knows" the unknown, but at other times he cautions against this very sort of claim. Jung's theory of individuation and the development of higher psychological functions through self-awareness is a model I want to preserve because of its unique contribution to understanding adults.

Yet I no longer believe that a universal Self unfolds through an inner process. I have gradually become convinced that selves are created and sustained in relationships, from birth to death. As philosopher Charles Taylor (1989) says in his book, *Sources of the Self*, "one is a self only among other selves. A self can never be described without reference to those who surround it" (p. 35). Like psychoanalyst D. W. Winnicott's famous dictum, "There's no such thing as a baby (only a baby and a mother)," I would like to say that there is no such thing as a self—only selves.

The state of being a unitary subject is sustained by ongoing experiences of coherence, the integration of complex subjective states into unity, and of continuity, the story of oneself over time and space. Coherence and continuity depend on human relationships. Our momentary integration is powerfully affected by emotional states (in which archetypal images arise, in my view) that organize or structure universal patterns of human interactions. Selves over time are not linked directly to these universal emotions, however. Selves are mediated by stories told by other selves. These are narratives about gender, class, or ethnic meanings. They are also cultural dictates for the general design of selves, such as degree of individuality, sense of inwardness, degree of boundedness, and so on.

Every self is embedded in a "symbolic order," as psychoanalyst Jacques Lacan calls the ongoing drama into which we are born. Some symbolic orders describe a self that is unique and individual with personal characteristics, while others describe a self that is collective, dependent entirely on the survival of the group—hence neither independent nor personally responsible. Gender is an important story for all selves, whether they are unique or collective. All cultures (with a few minor exceptions) divide people into two exclusive groups, marking every self both intrapsychically and interpersonally from birth to death.

To be a member of the human community is to be marked by a sign of female or male and the requirement to join one of two exclusive clubs. These two clubs are created on the principle of division, the division of the world into two sexes, and the requirements of gender applicable for each. This division in the symbolic order creates also an intrapsychic division between the identity marked as "self" and that marked as "other." In each one of us live both personalities, one of a conscious gendered self and another of a less conscious or unconscious contrasexual other (*contrasexual* means our opposite-sexed personality). Both are emotionally charged with images, habits, thoughts, actions and meanings that arise and are sustained in a matrix of relationships. The division of human beings into two genders is both the separation of gendered persons into two groups and the intrapsychic separation of the "I" from a "not-I" of the opposite sex.

What makes contrasexuality so powerful as an emotional determinant of development is its unique relationship with the self. The contrasexual other constrains and defines the self. The way I act and imagine myself as a woman carries with it a tandem meaning of what I imagine to be male and masculine, what I see as human but "not-woman." This develops into a subpersonality of a masculine other that is paradoxically the product of a female psyche. The same is true for the feminine other in the male psyche.

Before I go any further in describing these multiple subjectivities, I need to point out the difference between the terms *sex* and *gender* as I use them and to touch briefly on the role of envy between the sexes. Sex is the difference of embodiment, the structural and functional properties of the human body, that mean both possibilities and constraints on who we can be. Sex is definite and inflexible in most cases. It is "read" from the structure of the body and used to assign an infant into a gender group at birth. Sex provides particular biological possibilities. Breasts, vagina, vulva, womb, smaller body size, menstruation, pregnancy, lactation, menopause and greater longevity are expected of a female body. Penis, greater body size, greater physical strength, impregnation, and lesser longevity are expected of the male body. These and other biological differences (e.g., the structure of the brain and hormonal chemistry) limit us in our biological-sexual-reproductive possibilities. Although we may struggle against these limitations (e.g., by dressing like the other sex or attempting surgically to change the body), we cannot escape our embodiment. It will mold our lives forever.

Gender, on the other hand, is more flexible. Gender consists of the characteristics, social roles, personality traits, power, and status that are assigned by any society to each of the sexes. Gender serves many purposes in the way societies organize work and power so that the tasks of life can get done. Gender is more flexible than sex in the sense that it varies by context—group, family, society. In some societies, for example, men are expected to be more nurturing and home-oriented than women, taking care of the young. In others, like our North American societies, women are expected to be the primary caregivers. Most societies offer biological explanations for their gender meanings. No matter how gender characteristics may vary by society, most people believe they are carrying out some kind of biological "destiny."

One basic gender difference cuts across most known societies: women have less power than men. No matter what work women do or what characteristics are expected of them, they have less voice in decision-making and fewer privileges and rewards connected with their traits and roles. This is a fact. Often a biological explanation is used to explain this fact, e.g., that men are physically stronger than women. Whatever the explanation, this power difference between genders has vast psychological implications for development and individuation.

The biological differences of sex, and the power differences of gender, contribute to troubling emotions that arise in regard to the opposite sex. Envy, jealousy, idealization and fear are common feelings about the opposite sex. Intrapsychic barriers to development form around these emotions in both women and men. I will talk more about these in the last section of the paper.

At the moment, I want to address the most confusing of these troubling emotions, envy. Both sexes envy the biological resources of the other. Envy is a form of aggression or hate that expresses the desire to destroy what another possesses because one cannot possess it for oneself. Envy is an emotional attack that diminishes, empties, or belittles another in an effort to deal with the feelings of emptiness aroused by the other's resources. Each sex looks at the other's biologically ordained possibilities with the knowledge that these cannot be possessed by the self. Biological envy cannot be reduced to certain organs such as penis, breast or womb because it is a shifting drama, based on limitations (e.g., in the chronicity of mid-life illnesses, women see doctors six times more often than men and envy men's apparent health, but then men envy women's longevity in the average eight-year-longer life span of women).

What about envy of gender differences? Isn't it a simple matter of women envying men? It is certainly true that female people envy the greater privileges and freedoms afforded to male people, characterized by psychoanalyst Nancy Chodorow (1978) as "phallus envy." It is also true, though, that male people envy the lesser privileges (and what is imagined to be fewer responsibilities) connected with being female. Also, we North Americans are now in a peculiar situation in terms of the "men's movement(s)" which have evolved somehow in response to the "women's movement(s)." Many men seem to envy the clear and competent identities and emotional support and closeness that women have found among themselves in their searches for something better.

Envy of the biological possibilities and gendered power of the opposite sex limits our ability to see ourselves clearly and to empathize with the others. Jung's concept of the contrasexual personality, and especially its role in adult development, is a tool that I use clinically to pull apart the themes of sex, gender, and envy in the process of individuation through therapeutic work.

Before I discuss this, a brief word about the "mystical authoritarianism" of some Jungian concepts of gender differences. I now disagree completely with the assignment of universal principles of Masculine and Feminine to human development. In this model, women are expected to embody Eros or a natural relatedness, and men are expected to embody Logos or a natural rationality. Each is expected to develop the opposite for completion of the Self. The authority for making this kind of pronouncement comes from a reading of "archetype" that dictates human nature and development. I now read "archetype" to mean the predisposition to form certain universal images in emotionally charged states. There is no message here about how women and men should be or become. Although differences of embodiment confine each sex to certain experiences, the psychological implications of this confinement vary widely by context and culture. The complexity of human subjectivity embedded in a matrix of relationships cannot be captured by formulas.

When I wrote *Hags and Heroes* back in 1983, I saw things differently. From the work of feminist theorists like Nancy Chodorow (1978), Jean Baker Miller (1976), Dorothy Dinnerstein (1976) and others, I believed that men were by nature more autonomous/separate and women were more empathic/related. I accepted the explanation that early dependence on a female caregiver produced greater empathy in females and more autonomy in males. Since that time, I have come to see that these gendered styles of interaction depend more on context than on the influence of a female caregiver. By context, I mean the immediate surroundings and long-term socialization of a person's gender. Psychologist Eleanor Maccoby (1990) illustrates this in her recent report on twenty-five years of research on sex differences. She found essentially *no* individual differences of personality traits or intelligence to emerge between the sexes when they are measured on standard psychological tests. However, she also found that "expectable" differences in interactive styles emerge consistently *when the two sexes are together, either working or playing*. The two sexes do not significantly differ across hundreds of traits, but when they interact with each other, female people express themselves in more communal or related ways, and male people express themselves in more independent or autonomous ways. Something takes place when the two sexes are interacting that evokes the differences we expect from the symbolic order.

Keeping all of the above in mind, I would like to turn now to my definition of *individuation* from Jung's psychology. Although it is possible, and sometimes recommended, to link Jung's definition of individuation to a lifelong process of development, I am going to use the narrower meaning of the term. This is the process of recognizing and understanding one's own divided nature, the multiples of subjectivity that compete for control of oneself. Jung described individuation as a recognition of "psychic totality"—of inner conflicts and the balance of conscious and unconscious processes. This awareness, Jung believed, would permit a *disidentification* with complexes of childhood, a new viewpoint on attitudes that one initially took to be true and natural.

Self-dividedness often arises through neurosis—personal disillusionment, lack of agency, the inability to meet one's goals and desires no matter how hard one seems to try. Symptoms such as phobias or depression may interfere; wishes and fantasies may depose realistic goals; decision-making may seem impossibly impeded, and so on. As long as the parental complexes of childhood are the structures on which "reality" is situated, either by identifying with them or by projecting them onto others (especially the actual parents), a person is unable to feel this self-division. A person unable to be a "psychological individual" is not capable of self-reflection and personal meaning because beliefs are assumed to come from self-evident truths. Ask such a person "Why do you believe this?" and you are likely to hear the answer "Because it is true" without any awareness of another frame of reference.

Our culture invites neurosis to some extent, because we value diversity and individuality. There are cultures in which the collective code is more salient than the individual one. In these cultures, the process of individuation I am about to describe would not happen as it happens here. There would be no acute awareness of self-division nor a need for psychoanalysis. Adult development would occur through a more orderly process of tradition and ritual. Psychological awareness is a more chaotic or less orderly process through which we take responsibility for our own subjective states.

How do we function prior to this awareness? What happens to people who never fall into neurosis? People who never resolve neurosis? Prior to neurosis, and preventing neurosis, is identification with what Jung calls the "persona"— the psychological complex that functions *as if* one were a psychological individual. This is a Jungian version of what psychoanalyst D. W. Winnicott calls the "false self." Jung does not consider the persona to be originally pathological, but an ongoing identification with the persona over adulthood *can* lead to psychopathology or a personality that is one-dimensional.

In our society, the persona emerges most forcefully in adolescence with the pressure for a unique identity. Growing up, a child is repeatedly told how she/he looks, feels, is, and should be, especially in regard to gender. When self-searching adolescents ask themselves the question "Who am I?" they answer in terms of the persona—either in imitation of, or in opposition to, the values and ideals they have received from family and community. Under ordinary conditions, without childhood trauma, the persona functions in late adolescence and early adulthood as "only a mask of the collective psyche, a mask that *feigns indi-*

viduality, making others and oneself believe that one is individual" (CW 7, par. 245, italics in original).

In order to become a psychological individual, a person must break the identification with the persona and take responsibility for the multiple voices of subjectivity. If one is able to differentiate oneself from the "social look"—the way one wants to appear—one becomes aware of competing desires and moods in oneself. Then a person has the possibility of seeing through appearances.

As Jung puts it:

> Neurosis is self-division. In most people the cause of the division is that the conscious mind wants to hang on to its moral ideal, while the unconscious strives after its . . . unmoral ideal which the conscious mind tries to deny. (CW7, par. 18)

Neurotic conflict provokes loss of self-control. Then a person feels unable to bring actions into line with expectations. Such experiences introduce the possibility that one's subjectivity is more complex and less understood than one had previously imagined. Often this is the point at which a person seeks psychotherapy. (Let's leave open for discussion the question of whether or not neurosis is common today.)

The beginning of individuation is the development of *metacognitive* processes (thinking about one's thoughts, feelings and states) with the goal of looking at oneself from a "third" point of view. This "third" point of view is one that can see both consciousness and unconsciousness, but identifies with neither. One engages in a dialectical relationship with oneself and discovers that conscious strivings and unconscious impulses can both be understood as "the object of an unknown and supraordinate subject" (CW 7, par. 405).

Jung refers to this central supraordinate subject as the "self" or central organization of the personality. Experientially, one comes to feel able to witness and accept a range of subjective experiences in oneself without blame. The usual outcome of this witnessing includes greater courage, insight, and empathy, leading to new forms of creativity—forms that "can unite the opposites," as Jung says (CW 6, par. 185). This capacity to unite the opposites in one's being is what D. W. Winnicott calls "play" and what Jung calls the "transcendent function." It is the goal of successful analysis and an opening into further developments of complex subjectivity in the life of the analysand.

I have led you this far on definitions only, but I hope you are beginning to see that the move from neurosis to individuation can be affected by gender. In our society, people identify with the persona of adolescent masculinity or femininity and feel trapped into stereotyped roles: caregiving for females and independence for males. The neurotic breakdown of the persona looks very different for each gender because of the strong imposition of gender expectations in adolescence. Female people are usually encouraged to see themselves, especially in adolescence, as secondary to male people as they are prepared to be marginal in a society that regards their only legitimate power to be appearance. Even when they are encouraged to see themselves as equal (or better), they are confronted with the reality of limited status and decision-making. All North American women are faced with the "double bind of female authority": if they claim it directly, they will be considered to be "too much" (too emotional, too intellectual, too masculine or too weird); if they disclaim it, they will be forced to identify with being childlike and immaturely dependent in ways that will increase their anxiety about being separate individuals. No matter how a woman deals with her own authority, she will inevitably get it wrong because it *is* a double bind.

The experiencing of "getting it wrong" often leads women to the breakdown of the persona as they blame themselves for what has gone awry in their lives, or in the lives of their children and husbands. Self-blame and feelings of inferiority are the two most common neurotic issues that bring women to see me. In the case of otherwise healthy women, the double bind of female authority often opens the door to individuation.

The developmental task for a woman is then to recognize the disclaimed and excluded authority, competence, goodness, and power that have been assigned to the contrasexual other within and/or without. In traditional psychoanalytic jargon, this is often described as "increasing ego strength," but I see it as a task of breaking down the persona of childhood and gender-related complexes that justified and defended her feelings of self-blame or inferiority. When this happens successfully, a woman's self is enhanced by claiming the qualities that had been dissociated from it. A typical example is a mid-life woman who has one or several college degrees, is rearing a family, and works part-time, but who finds herself to be completely devoid of abilities and cannot make a decision about "what I want to do with the rest of my life." Often a situation like this includes an identification with a depressed and/or disabled mother complex, as well as the projection of her own authority and competence onto other men or women (who appear to have integrated authority). The claiming of the disclaimed masculine complex and differentiation from the mother complex are the tasks of individuation.

In adolescence especially, male people are encouraged to overestimate their abilities and possibilities. They tend to "see the world as their oyster." Young men may fall prey to an inflation of the persona and become narcissistic, defending themselves against any feelings of dependence on others. They may fall prey to an inflation of the ego and suffer manic, compulsive or anxiety states in competing to succeed. The persona of a young white man often means identifying with being strong, competent, and full of possibilities. The dissociated experiences of weakness, limitation, dependence, and personal need are then projected onto the opposite sex. Even when young men see themselves as sensitive, dependent and expressive, they still have a tendency to inflate these qualities with powerful significance (e.g., feeling "more sensitive" than others) because of the differential privilege and status of their position in the symbolic order.

Often it takes a man a decade or more of adulthood before this persona breaks down. In mid-life especially, many men feel sorely and painfully disappointed in what they have not achieved: recognition and friends they have not amassed, status and power they have failed to collect. Some men are confronted by their family members about what is missing in their relationships. These men feel a profound despair about ever finding the missing quality because of the inflated identification with the persona or ego. If they haven't yet got this magic quality, how could they now develop it? (The assumption here is that the man is "all" he can be and this is not "enough.")

In otherwise healthy men, the neurotic breakdown of

the persona usually includes depression in confronting what is missing. This confrontation brings about not a sense of self-blame (as with women), but a feeling of absolute despair. The gap between the inflated persona or ego and the feedback from current work or relationships seems impossibly large.

As I said earlier, the problem of envy exists as a barrier to further development in both sexes. Envy can function to disempower the self through identifying with the image of being empty of resources. In women, envy can be further complicated by feelings of self-pity in regard to inequality of power and privilege. Envy is complicated in men who are cut off from a social network of friends and relatives and feel that only their wives or lovers can connect them to such resources.

Envy often leads to trivializing or belittling people of the other gender (the therapist, spouse, parent, child) who confront one with shortcomings. Envy can fuel false comparisons of one's own and others' potentials, rights, and privileges. The first step in coming to terms with envy is recognizing the resources that belong to the self. A sense of resources replaces a sense of emptiness. This in itself may transform envy into jealousy, the desire to possess (instead of destroy) what the other seems to have, and this is a step in the direction of reclaiming one's own contrasexuality. The movement from envy to jealousy, from emptiness to resources, can be jeopardized in psychotherapy if the therapist fails to recognize the meanings of gender differences in individuation.

In individual psychotherapy or analysis, there are three levels in the therapeutic relationship in which sex and gender are critically important. The first is the helping relationship or the therapeutic alliance in which two people assess each other in terms of one person's ability to help the other. When looking for a therapist, people often request a therapist of their own sex. A same-sexed therapist may be more able to empathize, but this does not necessarily mean more effective therapeutic treatment— although it *may* mean it.

On the level of therapeutic expertise of the therapist, understanding sex and gender differences is critical for the initial assessment, mapping the stages of treatment and planning outcomes. My own and others' work on images of self and contrasexuality in dreams and fantasies are maps or models for assisting therapists in understanding both competent and pathological functioning that prescribe certain conditions (e.g., a holding environment versus an anxiety-provoking approach) at each stage of the treatment. These conditions are set and monitored by the therapist. A major error I have seen in supervising students and others is the therapist's inability to understand a "feminine persona" in a mid-life or older woman. The therapist may become patronizing or parental in a way that is insulting to the patient, if the therapist stereotypes the persona. The meaning of femininity in the patient's adolescence and the effect of the mother complex need to be assessed in this kind of persona. A feminine persona may be anything but a childlikeness in an older or mid-life woman. A feminine persona means many things, depending on the age cohort in which the woman grew up. It may represent a position of strength within the female community and one of negotiation in the world.

Responding to "therapeutic ruptures" is another critically important event in which sex and gender differences must be well understood by the therapist. A therapeutic rupture is a crisis in treatment in which the patient deeply doubts or questions the therapist's ability to be helpful. Accurate empathy or mirroring are the only vehicles for repairing such ruptures, in my view. My own work with men in individual treatment has taught me a great deal about maleness and its meanings in such moments of rupture. I have experienced, for example, the courage involved in being the major breadwinner in a family that rarely acknowledges this gift of love. I have felt this in empathizing with men who are afraid to ask for appreciation.

The third level is transferential discharge of unconscious psychological complexes. One young man was reworking with me his suffocating, idealizing mother complex. He was startled when I suggested that admiration and love are different. "Are they really different?" he said, and I quickly alerted myself to hear his question in a gendered context. Men tend genuinely to confuse the two because of their socialization and their relationships with mothers who admire them, especially as adolescents or adults. If a woman had asked this question, I would have listened in a different way because I would tend to believe the question was rhetorical, that she was pulling back from me because of something I had said or done.

Couple psychotherapy is another therapeutic environment in which psychological complexes are discharged. Couple psychotherapy is a powerful intervention when it can successfully provoke the breakdown of the persona or takes place after an initial neurosis has been resolved. It provides the opportunity to transform an intimate relationship into an arena for ongoing development through understanding and accepting differences. For heterosexual couples, this is primarily a process of claiming what is contrasexual in oneself and accepting the actual identity of one's partner. This is a progressive uncovering of the truths of both people and seeing the contexts in which they have developed. Being alert to sex and gender differences in any kind of therapy provides the possibility for moving beyond silencing and stereotyping of the opposite-sexed others, based on the disclaimed contrasexuality in ourselves.

This paper has been a brief excursion into expansive territory—what might be called the gendered themes of self and other as they assist or prevent individuation. I have only touched on a few of the myriad ways sex and gender mark our development. In the first two sections of the paper, I tried to show how Jung's theory of contrasexuality can be used to understand a gendered self without becoming "steeped . . . in phylogenetic, mystical authoritarianism." Recognizing that the experience of being a unitary subject, a self, is dependent on other selves, on a text and context in which we all participate, frees us from naming universals when we should be listening to people speak.

In the final section of the paper, I tried to show how vitally important it is for therapists and patients to understand sex and gender differences. The dyadic relationship of psychotherapy and the dyadic bond of adult attachment are charged with sexual and gendered meanings. To assure that these are relationships of love, not of power, we would do well to remember this description by poet Adrienne Rich (1990): "An honorable human relationship —that is, one in which two people have the right to use the word love—is a process, delicate, violent, often terrifying to both persons involved, a process of refining the truths they can tell each other" (p. 3). When a therapeutic relationship or an adult attachment bond leads to individuation, we encounter such a process of "refining the truths" we can tell, especially in regard to the meanings of sex and gender.

Chodorow, N. 1978. *The Reproduction of Mothering: Psychoanalysis and the Sociology of Gender*. Berkeley, Calif.: University of California Press.

Dinnerstein, D. 1976. *The Mermaid and the Minotaur: Sexual Arrangements and Human Malaise*. New York: Harper and Row.

Maccoby, E. 1990. Gender and Relationships: A Developmental Account. *American Psychologist* 45 (4): 513-520.

Miller, J. B. 1976. *Toward a New Psychology of Women*. Boston: Beacon Press.

Rich, A. 1990. *Women and Honor: Some Notes on Lying*. Pittsburgh: Cleis Press.

Seidenberg, R. 1991. Psychoanalysis and Femininity II. *Psychoanalytical Psychology* 8(2): 225-237.

Taylor, C. 1989. *Sources of the Self*. Cambridge, Mass.: Harvard University Press.

The King and the Corpse: An Ancient Parable for a Modern Predicament

STEPHEN MARTIN

This paper represents both a pleasure and a burden. A pleasure because there is no greater contribution, as far as I am concerned, that C. G. Jung has made to the understanding of personal psychological development than his concept of individuation. But it is a burden also because describing individuation is like trying to describe life itself. How are we to make really clear what it means to "become what one most innately is," or to "become completely individual and differentiated from the collective," or to "integrate all the parts of the psyche." Nevertheless, as we are all "individuators," I am going to give it a try, both literally and symbolically, in order to provide some overview of it. Goodness knows we need all the help with our process that we can get. The structure I will follow is simple: I would first like to highlight what I consider to be four important characteristics of individuation, and then explore a teaching story, an Indian fairy tale entitled "The King and the Corpse," that captures something of each.

Jung first introduced the term *individuation* in 1916, in a lecture, "Adaptation, Individuation, Collectivity"

(CW 18, par. 1084-1106), that lay unpublished in hidden archives in Zürich for fifty years. In this paper, he outlined his basic thinking about individuation by saying that in the course of life we sacrifice who and what we really are for the sake of adaptation to the standards, morality and conventions of our home culture.

This adaptation is what one might call the successful navigation of the "first half of life," a period of time when worldly concerns, such as identity formation, career, family and the like take precedence over all others. The price paid for this adaptation is formidable and by nature eventuates in imbalances in psychological life. We cannot develop in one direction without sacrificing others. Most frequently, however, these imbalances coalesce and become problematic at critical transition points, the most famous of which has come to be known now, in user-friendly terms, as "the mid-life crisis."

Even though conformity and adaptation to life and society—or in psychological terms, persona and basic ego development—are necessary evils, sooner or later, who we are, what we must be, what our individual destiny is and what our relationship to the timeless values of life is, become more and more important. Often, whether we like it or not, we are launched on a more conscious process of self-discovery and self-development. In my mind, this is what Jung defined as individuation.

Please note, I am electing to speak of individuation as a conscious endeavor, a task we undertake with eyes open and focused awareness, often in therapy, in creative work, and in meaningful suffering or on spiritual quests. This is to be distinguished from normal "unconscious individuation," or that process of natural psychological evolution that occurs even if the individual remains for all intent and purposes asleep. It is an open and interesting question whether consciously quickened and experienced individuation differs from "unconscious individuation." I have the impression that they are quite different.

There are four broad characteristics that can orient us in our discussion of individuation. The first, and perhaps the most central, is that in individuation there is an actively experienced dialogue between consciousness and the unconscious, or in other words between our sense of identity, who we are, the "persona/ego" part of us, and the continually emerging unknown within. This dialogue takes place all the time and in every phase of life, as an ongoing discussion to which we are privy, which critiques and comments on what we are feeling, how we are affected by inner and outer events, and what our relationships and responsibilities mean to us and say about us. This dialogue is in fact the basis of psychological-mindedness and is familiar to us all.

At critical times in life, we are often forced to look at this ongoing dialogue more closely and listen to it more attentively. We have to explore more thoroughly the character, the quality and the content of this relationship we have with our hidden selves. The periods when this is demanded are usually emotionally upsetting and involve suffering, a kind of rupture in the finely tuned and consistent fantasy we have of who we are. At such junctures, the entire inner family of complexes, archetypal images, errant feelings and emotions seems to revolt, overthrowing the fragile sovereignty of the "I" in favor of the cacophonous, albeit creative, chaos of unconscious arousal. At important times like this, our dialogue with our unknown selves is the most real reality we have.

Such an unconscious arousal points the way to the second characteristic of individuation—the fact that a differentiation of the inner world occurs when we pay active attention to it. Dialoguing with our unknown selves demands, as a rule, the deliberate withdrawal of projections from those around us, and from the world at large. By constantly asking the questions "Who am I in that? Where am I in that? Who is in that?" we quickly appreciate that we are many selves, many different people, part and whole, which formerly had been hidden in our perceptions of and opinions about other people and about life. From an intrapsychic perspective, when conscious individuation is undertaken, we come to realize that our dream and fantasy worlds are alive with part personalities, human and inhuman, animal and vegetable, weird and pedestrian, of which we were unaware. As we take our inner lives seriously, as symbolic of the progress we are making toward becoming who we are destined to be, the truth of the polymorphism within grows, and any notion of being a unified "me" diminishes.

Yet even when we recognize this polymorphism, this "many-ness," we hold onto the notion of our singularity, of our "I-ness." This leads us to the third consideration when thinking about individuation: the paradox of the unity amidst the multiplicity. To the uninitiated, the notion of differentiating the unconscious by giving voice and expressive value to the many parts sounds like an invitation to a dissociative state such as "multiple personality" or worse, to a rollicking case of schizophrenia, or the fragmentation of the personality. This is primarily because of the culturally dominant monotheistic fantasy that health is equivalent to oneness. Granted, any serious reader of Jung would point out the many places where he speaks of the ideal of personal development as becoming "oneself," or "whole," or— god help us—

"integrated," all of which are presided over by what he called the "Self," capital S.

Nevertheless, we also know from him, and from those who followed, that the psyche is plural, populated by the many within, the "little people of our complexes," the gods and goddesses. Who hasn't felt the sense of sublime oneness in the face of nature, or the experience of incredible many-ness when confronted with passionate ambivalences? In light of these opposing but equally palpable realities, what are we to make of this paradox? Many have speculated and advanced ingenious explanations, all of which I would like to boil down to a useful working hypothesis: our psyches are born out of a preconscious oneness and differentiate throughout our lives, always shadowed by the unseen yet palpable oneness. In the work of individuation, that oneness, that felt sense that all the parts are somehow connected, comes ever more to the forefront of experience, framing, gathering and relating the many within to each other, thus creating an ongoing experience of unity amidst the multiplicity that is characterized by a profound sense of meaning, destiny and purpose.

This leads me to the fourth and final characteristic. Individuation is a process and not a goal. Often I have asked myself, what does an individuated person look like? Was Jung an example, or some of his long-lived students and colleagues? How could they have been individuated given their flaws, uncertainties, their obvious and sometimes embarrassing humanity? Are individuated persons perfect, don't they "glow in the dark"? The answer to this question is, of course, obvious. No individual arrives at maximum differentiation or achieves a permanent integration of all his/her parts.

Long ago, Heraclitus, the patron pre-Socratic saint of Jungian thought, meant it when he said, "You would not find out the boundaries of the soul, even by traveling along every path, so deep a measure does it have," and Paul Klee, my patron saint, expressed it in his own way in the 1920s, when he wrote that "becoming is more important than being."

To put it bluntly, the dialogue with the unconscious, the differentiation of our inner worlds, and the evolution of a sense of personal meaning and purpose never cease. Instead, through whatever form of self-reflection or consciousness-making an individual develops, in whatever manner or style that suits, symbols—the fruit of the dialogue and differentiation of which we speak—continue to flower in the form of dreams and fantasies, artwork or creative thought. And by definition, individuation continues to go on. The "doing" is the reward, a doing without end, illuminating endless possibilities of meaning that can continually deepen life and which can lead to the only by-product of individuation that I can see, namely, wisdom. I define this wisdom as the humble certainty that one knows nothing but welcomes all and everything with equal grace. To me, wisdom presides over the gathering of selves that we call individuation by enabling the ego, our "I-ness," to know its place amongst the assembled parts and, rather than feeling displaced or diminished, allows it to feel a partner in the marvelous experience of meaning.

With this fourfold orientation in mind, let me comment on an oft-told and much loved Hindu fairy tale, "The King and the Corpse," which was brought to the attention of Western audiences by Heinrich Zimmer, the great Indologist and friend of Jung. As it unfolds, this story has much to tell us about these four characteristics of individuation.

The King and the Corpse

as told by
HEINRICH ZIMMER*

It was remarkable, the way the king became involved in the adventure. For ten years, every day, there had been appearing in his audience chamber, where he sat in state hearing petitions and dispensing justice, a holy man in the robe of a beggar ascetic, who, without a word, would offer him a fruit. And the royal personage would accept the trifling present, passing it along without an afterthought to his treasurer standing behind the throne. Without making any request, the mendicant would then withdraw and vanish into the crowd of petitioners, having betrayed no sign either of disappointment or of impatience.

Then it happened one day, some ten years after the first appearance of the holy man, that a tame monkey, having escaped from the women's apartments in the inner palace, came bounding into the hall and leaped upon the arm of the throne. The mendicant had just presented his gift, and the king playfully handed it over to the monkey. When the animal bit into it, a valuable jewel dropped out and rolled across the floor.

The king's eyes grew wide. He turned with dignity to the treasurer at his shoulder. "What has become of all the others?" he asked. But the treasurer was unable to say. He had been tossing the unimpressive gifts through an upper, trellised window into the treasure house, not even bothering to unlock the door. And so he excused himself and hurried to the vault. Opening it, he made his way to the part beneath the little window. There, on the floor, lay a mass of rotten fruit in various stages of decay and, amidst this debris of many years, a heap of priceless gems.

The king was pleased, and

---

* From Heinrich Zimmer. *The King and the Corpse*.

he bestowed the entire heap upon the treasurer. Of a generous spirit, he was not avid for riches, yet his curiosity was aroused. Therefore when the ascetic next morning presented himself, tendering in silence his apparently modest offering, the king refused to accept it unless he would pause awhile and speak. The holy man stated that he wished an interview in private. The king granted the desire, and the mendicant at last presented his request.

What he required, he told the king, was the help of a hero, a truly intrepid man, to assist in an enterprise of magic.

The king was interested in hearing more.

The weapons of true heroes, the magician explained, are renowned in the annals of magic for their peculiar exorcising powers.

The king permitted his petitioner to continue.

The stranger thereupon invited him to come, on the night of the next new moon, to the great funeral ground, where the dead of the city were cremated and the criminals hanged.

The king, undaunted, gave assent; and the ascetic—who bore the appropriate name of "Rich in Patience"—took his leave.

The appointed night arrived: the night of the next new moon. The king, alone, girded on his sword, wrapped himself in a dark mantle, and with muffled countenance set forth on the questionable adventure. As he approached the dreadful burial ground, he became increasingly aware of the tumult of the specters and demons hovering about the uncanny place, feasting upon the dead, and celebrating their horrible carousals. Fearlessly he continued. When he crossed into the burning-area, by the light of the still smoldering funeral pyres his alert eyes half discerned, half guessed, the charred scattering of the blackened skeletons and skulls. His ears throbbed to the hideous uproar of the ghouls.

He proceeded to the rendezvous, and there was his sorcerer, intently drawing a magic circle on the ground.

"Here I am," the king said. "What can I do for you?"

The other hardly lifted his eyes. "Go to the other end of the burning ground," he said, "and you will find the corpse of a hanged man dangling from a tree. Cut it down and bring it here."

The king turned, and crossing again the extensive area, came to a giant tree. The moonless night was illuminated only by the dim flickering of the exhausted pyres; the goblins made an inhuman din. Yet he was unafraid, and perceiving the hanged man dangling there, he ascended the tree and cut the rope with his sword. When the corpse fell, it gave a moan, as though it had been hurt. The king, thinking there must still be life in it, began to grope over the rigid form. A shrill laugh broke from its throat, and the king realized that the body was inhabited by a ghost.

"What are you laughing at?" he demanded.

The instant he spoke, the corpse flew back to the limb of the tree.

The king ascended and again cut the body down. He lifted it without a word this time, placed it on his shoulder, and began to walk. But he had not taken many steps when the voice in the corpse began to speak. "O King, let me shorten the way for you with a tale," it said. The king did not reply, and so the spirit told its story.

There was, once upon a time, a certain prince who went on a hunting party with a young friend; the friend was the son of the chancellor of the prince's father. And losing touch with their companions, they strolled aimlessly through the forest, until they arrived at a pleasant lake where they paused to rest. The prince saw a beautiful maiden bathing on the farther bank, who, unobserved by her companions, was already making signals to him across the water. He was unable to understand the signs, but the chancellor's son was catching their meaning very well. She had communicated her name, that of her family, and that of the kingdom in which she lived, and was announcing her love. When she turned and vanished into the foliage, the two youths at last got up and ambled home.

Another day, under the pretext of another hunting party, the two friends set off again into the jungle, detached themselves, and went to the town in which the girl lived. They found lodging in the house of an old woman, whom they bribed to serve as messenger. The girl was so cunning that she was able to formulate a reply which the old woman did not recognize as the arrangement of a rendezvous. The signals were deciphered by the clever son of the chancellor. Then, for lunar reasons, the rendezvous had to be postponed, and the girl described, again by signals, how the prince might climb into her father's garden and ascend to her lofty chamber. He entered, as arranged, through her window, and the two young lovers found delight in each other's arms.

The girl was both passionate and cunning. When she learned that her signals had been deciphered not by the prince but by his friend, she was immediately afraid that her affair would be betrayed, and so she determined to poison the interpreter. He, however, was her match, and had even foreseen that this would come to pass. He had devised a plan that would teach her, once and for all, that he knew how to take care both of himself and of his prince.

The young man disguised himself as a beggar ascetic, persuaded the prince to play the role of the ascetic's pupil, and then, by a clever stratagem, brought the girl into suspicion as a witch. He convinced the king of the country that she had been the cause of the recent sudden death of his infant son, and he produced such proof that she was condemned to a disgraceful death. Exposed naked outside of the town, she was left prey to the beasts of the surrounding jungle. But the moment she was abandoned, the two young men, having procured swift horses for themselves, snatched her up and fled with her to the prince's realm, where she became his bride and future queen. Grief over the disgrace and loss overcame the aged parents of the maid; their hearts broke and they died.

"Now who was guilty of the death of those two?" suddenly demanded the specter in the corpse. "If you know the answer and do not reply, your head will burst into a hundred pieces."

The king believed that he knew the answer, but suspected that if he uttered a word the corpse would go flying back to the tree. Nevertheless, he did not wish his head to explode.

"Neither the maid nor the prince was guilty," he said, "because they were inflamed by the arrows of love. Nor was the son of the chancellor guilty, for he was not acting upon his own responsibility but in the service of his master. The only one guilty was the king of that country, who let such things come to pass within his realm. He did not see through the subtle trick played on the natural grief that he felt for his infant son. He failed to note that the mien of the beggar ascetic was no more than a disguise. He had never taken cognizance of the activities of the two strangers in his capital; he was not even aware that they were there. Therefore, he is to be judged guilty of failure in his kingly duty, which was to be the all-seeing eye of his kingdom, the all-knowing protector and governor of his folk."

When the last word of the judgment had left the speaker's tongue, the burden, groaning in mock agony, vanished from his back, and he knew that it was hanging again from the arm of the tree. He returned, cut the corpse down, shouldered the load, and tried again.

"My dear sir," said the voice, addressing him anew, "you have encumbered yourself with a difficult and curious charge. Permit me to while the time away for you with a pleasant tale.

"Now, once upon a time there were three young Brahmins who had lived a number of years in the home of their spiritual teacher. All three had fallen in love with their teacher's daughter, and he did not dare to bestow her on any one of them for fear of breaking the others' hearts. But then the maid was stricken with a serious illness and died, and the three young men, equally desperate, committed her body to a funerary pyre. When it had been cremated, the first decided to give vent to his grief by wandering through the world as a beggar ascetic, the second gathered the beloved bones from among the ashes and proceeded with them to a celebrated sanctuary beside the life-giving waters of the holy Ganges, while the third, remaining on the spot, constructed a hermit's hut over the place of the fire, and slept on the ashes of the body of his love.

"Now the one who had decided to roam through the world was one day the witness of an extraordinary event. He saw a man read from a book a magic charm that restored a child to life whose body had already been consumed to ashes. Stealing the book, the young lover hurried back to the cremation scene, and arrived just when the one who had gone to the Ganges also returned, the latter having dipped the bones into the life-giving stream. The skeleton was reassembled among the ashes, the charm was read from the book, and the miracle came to pass. The thrice-beloved arose again, more beautiful than ever. So at once the rivalry was resumed, but more hotly now; for each claimed to have earned the right to her: one having guarded her ashes, one having dipped her bones in the Ganges, and the third having pronounced the spell.

"And so to whom does she belong?" said the voice in the corpse. "If you know the answer but do not reply, your head will explode."

The king believed he knew, and so was forced to reply. "The one who recalled her to life with the magic spell and had little trouble in doing so is her father," he said, "and the one who rendered the pious service to her bones fulfilled the duty of a son. But the one who slept on the ashes, did not depart from her, and devoted his life to her, may be termed her spouse."

A wise enough judgment—yet the moment it was given, the corpse was gone. Doggedly, the king returned, cut it down, and started again the unrewarding walk. The voice resumed. The king was given another riddle to solve, and again compelled to retrace his path. And so it went, time after time, the unrelenting specter in the corpse spinning tale upon tale of twisted destinies and tangled lives, while the king was driven to and fro. All of life with its joys and horrors was described. And the threads of the fantasies always twisted into knots of right and wrong, tangles of conflicting claims.

There was a story, for example, of the posthumous son of a thief, who was faced by a delicate problem when he went to make an offering to his dead father at a sacred well. His grandmother had been left a widow while still very young; and since her relatives had defrauded her of the inheritance, she had been compelled to go out into the world with only her little daughter. The night of her departure from the village, she came upon a thief who had been impaled and was on the verge of death. In terrible agony, hardly able to breathe, he expressed a desire to marry the little daughter, then and there—with the thought that the marriage would give him spiritual rights over her future son, even though the latter should be engendered by another, and this son then would be eligible to make the offerings due to the soul of a deceased father. In compensation, he would tell where he had concealed a certain stolen treasure.

The marriage was concluded in an informal though binding manner, the thief died, and the mother and daughter had a considerable fortune. The girl fell in love, in due time, with a handsome young Brahmin, and he consented to become her lover but insisted on a payment, because there was a certain courtesan whose fee he wished to be able to pay. The young woman conceived a son, and following the instructions of a dream, deposited the babe, together with a thousand gold pieces, at the threshold of the palace of a certain king. Now this king, who was without offspring and desirous of an heir to the throne, had happened that very night to dream that a child was about to be deposited at his door. He accepted the sign, and brought up the foundling as his son and heir.

Many years later, when the benevolent king had died, the young prince, incumbent to the throne, went to make an offering to his departed father. He proceeded to a holy well, where the dead were accustomed to stretch forth their hands to receive the proffered gifts. But instead of a single hand, three hands appeared to take his oblation: that of the impaled thief, that of the Brahmin, and that of the king. The prince did not know what to do. Even the priests attending the offering were at a loss. "Well," challenged the specter in the corpse, "into which hand should the prince consign his oblation?"

Again threatened with the explosion of his skull, the king pronounced judgment: "The oblation should be placed in the hand of the thief, for neither the Brahmin who begot the child nor the king who reared him has any valid claim. The Brahmin sold himself. The king received his compensation in the gold pieces. The man who made it possible for the prince to be born was the thief; his treasure paid for both the begetting and the fosterage. Furthermore, the thief had title to the child by marriage." Immediately, the corpse was off, and still another walk brought the king back to the tree.

Then there is that curious tale of the transposed heads, the tale of two lifelong friends and a girl. The maid married one of the two, but the marriage was not particularly happy. Shortly following the wedding, the couple, together with their bachelor friend, set forth on a visit to the parents of the bride. On the way, they came to a sanctuary of the bloodthirsty goddess Kali, and the husband excused himself, for a moment, to go into the temple alone. There, in a sudden excess of emotion, he decided to offer himself to the image as a sacrifice, and, with a keen-edged sacrificial sword that was there, lopped his head from his shoulders and collapsed in a pool of blood. The friend, having waited with the bride, went into the temple to see what had happened, and when he beheld the sight was inspired to follow suit. At last the bride came in, only to take flight again, intent on hanging herself from the limb of a tree. The voice of the goddess commanded her to halt, however, and sent her back to restore the lives of the two young men by replacing the heads. But because of her distraction, the young woman made the interesting mistake of putting the friend's head on the husband's body, and the husband's on the friend's. "To which now does she belong?" demanded the specter in the corpse, "the one with the husband's body, or the one with the husband's head?"

The king thinks he knows, and, to keep his own head from bursting, gives his answer: "The one with the husband's head; for the head ranks supreme among the members, just as woman among life's delights."

Again the corpse has vanished and again the king is trudging back to the fateful tree.

In all, twenty-four riddles are propounded; and the king can announce a solution to all but the last.

This last concerns the case of a father and son. They were members of a hill tribe of huntsmen, the father a chief. And the two had gone out on a hunting party, when they happened on the footprints of two women. Now the father was a widower and the son as yet unmarried, but the father in his sorrow for his deceased wife had rejected every suggestion that he should rewed. Still, the footmarks were particularly charming: the practiced eyes of the hunters judged that they had been left by a noble mother and daughter, fugitives of some aristocratic house—perhaps even a queen and a princess. The larger prints suggested the beauty of the queen and the smaller ones the fascination of the princess. The son was very much excited. But the father had to be persuaded. What the son proposed was that the father should marry the woman of the larger footprints and himself the smaller, as befitted their rank and age. He had to argue the point for some time, but at last the chieftain acquiesced, and the two took a solemn oath that that was the way it should be.

Then they made haste along the trail. And they came, at length, upon the two unhappy creatures, a queen and princess indeed—just as the tribesmen had suspected—in anxious flight from a situation that had developed at home when the king had unexpectedly died. But there was this disillusioning complication: the daughter was the one who had the larger feet. According to their oath, therefore, the son would be forced to marry the queen.

Father and son conducted their quarry into their mountain village, and there made wives of them; the daughter became the wife of the chief, and the mother of the son. Then the two women conceived.

"Now just how were the two male children that were born related to each other?" asked the voice of the specter in the corpse. "Precisely what was each to the other, and precisely what were they not?"

The king, carrying his burden, was unable to find any unequivocal term for this complicated relationship. The enigma had at last been found that could strike him dumb. And so he walked along with a remarkably buoyant stride, bemusing the problem in silence. The children would be living paradoxes of interrelationship, both this and that: uncle and nephew, nephew and uncle, at once on the father's side and on the mother's. . . .

Driven back into the problem of his own character and present predicament, he walked in silence, but with an admirable nimbleness of step that seemed heedless of the night's long ordeal. And apparently the specter was impressed, for when the voice spoke again, it was altered to a tone of respect.

"Sir," it said, "you seem cheerful in spite of all this weird tramping back and forth across the funeral ground; you are unafraid. I am pleased by the spectacle of your determination. You may have this corpse, therefore. Take it with you. I am about to quit it."

But this was not the end.

Before taking its departure, the voice warned that the projects of the magician ascetic were of terrible danger to them both; beneath the holy garment of renunciation throbbed a boundless lust for power and blood. The necromancer was about to use the king in a great enterprise of black magic, first as accomplice and then as a living human sacrifice.

"Listen, O King," the specter warned, "listen to what I have to tell you, and, if you value your own good, do exactly as I say.

"That beggar monk is a very dangerous imposter. With his powerful spells he is going to force me to re-enter this corpse, which he will then use as an idol. What he plans to do is to place it in the center of his magic circle, worship me there as a divinity, and, in the course of the worship, offer you up as the victim. You will be ordered to fall down and do me reverence, first on your knees, then prostrate, in the most slavish attitude of devotion, with your head, hands, and shoulders touching the ground. He will attempt then to decapitate you with a single stroke of your own sword.

"There is only one way to escape. When you are ordered to go down, you must say: 'Please demonstrate this slavish form of prostration, so that I, a king unused to such attitudes, may see how one assumes such a posture of worship.' And when he is lying flat on the ground, strike off his head with a quick cut of the sword. In that instant, all the supernatural power that this sorcerer is trying to conjure from the sphere of the celestials will fall to you. And you will be a potent king indeed!"

The specter, with that, departed and the king proceeded freely on his way. The magician betrayed no impatience at having been forced to wait, but on the contrary seemed filled with admiration that the task should have been accomplished at all. He had used the time to complete the ritual arrangement of his magic circle. It was all marked out with a hideous material gathered from the immediate neighborhood: a kind of paste composed of the whitish meal of ground bones mixed with the blood of dead bodies. And the area was unpleasantly alight with the flickering of wicks burning with corpse fat.

The sorcerer lifted the burden from the king's shoulder, washed it, and decorated it with garlands, as though it were a sacred image, then set it in the center of the magic circle. He summoned the specter by means of a series of potent incantations and compelled it to enter into the prepared body. Then he undertook to pay it worship after the manner of a priest paying worship to a divinity which has been invited to take up residence within a sacred image as an august guest. The time came, presently, for him to make the king go down, first on his knees, then on his face; but when he pronounced the command, his noble acolyte required to be shown how to take the posture. So the terrible monk got down on his knees. The king watched and waited. The monk fell forward, pressing his hands, shoulders and face to the ground, and with a quick slash the king struck off his head. The blood gushed. The king rolled the body over and with another expert blow split the chest. He ripped the heart out and offered it up, together with the head, as an oblation to the specter in the corpse.

Then a mighty sound of jubilation arouse out of the night from every side, from the host of surrounding spirits, souls, and ghouls, lifting a tumult of acclaim to the victor. By his deed he had redeemed the supernatural from the threat of the necromancer, who had been on the very point of reducing them all to slavery and enchantment.

The specter in the corpse lifted its uncanny voice, but now in joy and praise. "What the necromancer sought was absolute power over souls and ghouls," it said, "and over all the spiritual presences of the supernatural domain. That power now shall be yours, O King, when your life on earth is ended. I have tormented you; I shall therefore now make atonement. What do you wish? Announce your desire and it shall be granted."

The king asked, in compensation for his toils during this strangest of all the nights he had ever known, that the twenty-four riddle tales told him by the specter, together with the story of the night itself, should be made known over the whole earth and remain eternally famous among men.

The specter promised. "And furthermore," the voice stated, "not only shall the twenty-four tales be universally celebrated, but even Shiva, the Great God, Overlord of all the Specters and Demons, the Master-Ascetic of the Gods, will himself do them honor. Neither ghosts nor demons shall have any power, whenever and wherever these tales are told. And whoever recites with sincere devotion even a single one of them shall be free from sin."

With this promise the specter abruptly departed; and immediately Shiva, the Lord of the Universe, appeared in glory, attended by a multitude of gods. He gave greeting to the king and serenely thanked him, with high praise, for his deliverance of the powers of the spirit world from the impure hands of the aspiring ascetic. The divinity declared that the cosmic powers now were placed in the service of the king in return for his having prevented their misuse by the black magician who had been working for universal dominion, that the king would come into full possession of them at the close of his earthly career, and that during his lifetime he would govern the earth. Shiva bestowed upon him, with his own hand, the divine sword "Invincible," which should give him the sovereignty of the world; and then he lifted the veil of ignorance that had been concealing from his consciousness the immortal essence of his human life.

Blessed with this illumination, the king was free to take his leave of the gruesome proving ground. The dawn was breaking as he returned into the spacious halls of his lordly palace, like someone awakening from a night of troubled sleep. . . . During the following years the miraculous fulfillment of the splendor promised came to pass, and his earthly life was enlarged in virtue and glory.

Our story opens with a mighty king dispensing justice impartially and, as we might note, quite unconsciously, for the tale tells us that although every day, for some ten years, an unassuming beggar ascetic made him a "trifling present," this gesture went uninvestigated. Without an afterthought, the king passes on his modest gift to the impersonal machinery of state. As fairy tales are, according to Marie-Louise von Franz, the best way to study the comparative anatomy of the psyche, it is not hard to realize that this king represents the self-centered, self-involved and inflatedly unconscious part of our psyches, the persona-ego that reigns over life as if all were clear, all were in order, and all were sensible and explicable. At the cusp of the first and second half of life, this is who we usually think of ourselves as being, fully secure in the illusion of stable identity. Such a persona-ego is unaware of the mystery hidden within the fruits of daily life and is enthralled instead by the routine performance of duty and by meeting external expectations. In a word, this king has no conscious relationship to the unconscious, to the unknown parts of himself.

Unfailingly, it is at such unexpected moments, when one is least expecting it, that mischief occurs. The tables are turned and an uncontrolled, uncivilized "animal" part of ourselves, one of those inner inhabitants to whom we pay little attention, escapes its handlers (or our defenses) and forces us to look at what we have disregarded. Kings and royalty have monkeys around (or dwarfs) to parody human virtues and qualities as they scamper lustily and playfully around the courts of our souls. Monkeys are our libertarian, impulsive sides, our emotional selves that recognize only the natural law of curiosity and hunger for experience. When we remain kingly, the mere fruit of life is beneath us, saving ourselves as we do for more sophisticated treats. But to the monkey within, the imp who opens our purses and sometimes our buttons or zippers, these mundane things are indescribably delicious. The dialogue with the unknown is made possible and the jewel within revealed only by the monkey.

Confronted with his oversight, the king comes to know the ascetic "Rich in Patience", and engages in what Jung called the dialogue with the shadow. The king, the most powerful in the world of consciousness—persona-ego personified, if you will—meets his counterpart in the world of the occult, or of unconscious knowledge. In terms of individuation, the king must come to know the ascetic, because until he does so, he will remain unaware of and excluded from his own deeper nature. Before the appearance of the ascetic, it is as if nothing exists but what we, in our egocentricity, can see or touch. Often in therapy one encounters similiar experiences when the client is forced into a numinous confrontation with an unexpected other, perhaps in the form of an illness, or symptom, or an amorous passion, an other that has been knocking at the door for years. Suddenly all is not what it seems to be, and what once seemed to be under control is no longer. The ascetic becomes the king's guide to his own unknown inner domain, the doorway to his more conscious involvement in his own development. The appearance of the ascetic conforms to the first point of orientation of individuation.

The task set for the king is odd, indeed; it is to enter the realm of the dead, a hellish place of forgotten souls, rotting bodies and sepulchral lights, during the dark night of the new moon. It is as if the king must enter a place of inversion, where he is the servant instead of king, where darkness rules instead of the light of consciousness, where decomposition or regression rather than progression is the norm, and where pandemonium replaces good government. For the king to be in this world is for him to meet the stranger within himself, to meet his own dark potential.

What is fascinating about this tale and marks it as different from other tales that do not, I think, touch the heart of individuation quite as well, has to do with where the heroes and heroines must go. More frequently, the hero or heroine must enter magical lands or jeweled palaces, fascinating, marvelous and indescribably beautiful inner places, in order to propel the narrative onward. This tale is rather more mature, mirroring as it does how our playful lusts or desires can reveal the power and darkness that stands behind appearances. This tale is an underworld journey, a *nekyia* or descent into hell (like that of Inanna).

When one consciously engages the process of individuation, the harmless always reveals our ignorance of the true meaning of life and how critical it is that it be pursued, no matter how frightening or dangerous. Thus it makes perfect sense that the king must enter the funerary grounds which represent the graveyard of lost life, of sins and failings, of the unholy din of life unfulfilled or misunderstood. In a way, the king, who stands for our most coherent sense of ourselves, must enter a period of frightening confrontation with what has died within us, amidst the screams of the personalities and the half-light of smoldering desires within our unconscious world. Is this not the reason why most dreams in depth therapy are unnerving and strange? Is it not because we are forced to go deep in order to redeem our unfulfilled selves?

This confrontation with dead things that is forced upon us by our shadowy guide—that other self who lives another sort of life while we reach for the safety of identity and the security of our place in the world—is most dramatically portrayed in the image of the hanging corpse. What is denied congeals in the body of the corpse, until it finally becomes the housing for the spirit of all that we are not, which eventually bursts upon the scene mockingly, demanding conscious recognition. This spirit symbolizes the possessive power of the unrecognized unconscious, which can emotionally overwhelm conscious life with doubt, anxieties, odd thoughts, and fantasies, unmaking normal everyday life.

What ensues is a marvelous depiction of the dialogue between persona-ego consciousness and an animated inner world. The tale quickly dispels the notion that encountering the unconscious is a passive task, a burden to be borne and endured. On the contrary, this is not so. The moment the king cuts down the corpse, his strange interactive education begins. Instead of riding quietly and obediently on the king's shoulder, the corpse and its spirit familiar become illuminating tutors. During this long, bizarre night, the spirit within relates to the king twenty-four mind-breaking riddles, life's quintessence if you will, that test his reason and his judgment, those very factors that define his kingship.

What does this tell us about individuation? If the corpse symbolizes our suspended failings, our forgotten and repressed life that we are forced to bypass during our long road to adaptation, the spirit's insoluble stories are dramatic examples of the limitation of our persona-ego vision. For although all through life we may feel that we have made the right decisions, in this underworld where all is inverted and on its head, nothing is so simple. In effect, we are damned if we do, damned if we don't. When confronted with the underside of life, there is no certainty. When forced to see in the half-light of inference and of lost opportunity, reason comes to a full and humiliating stop.

In these tales of confusion, deceit, treachery, possession, desire, devotion, attachment and status—components of normal everyday shadowy reality—the king is forced to confront his own process of reasonable judgment. One has the feeling that no matter what he might answer it would be wrong, for it is only part of the picture. Is not the spirit's true purpose to parade before the king life in all its contrary, idiosyncratic, and ineffable fullness, in order to challenge his smug notion that he has everything under control? In this kingdom, reason and logic, tools of kingship, do not reign. These stories are nothing less than the images of his own inner kingdom, the different parts of himself that cannot be categorized, adjudicated and assigned to their particular compartments.

Each time that the king attempts an answer—granted, in fear that his head might explode (which we realize is nothing less than the desired end)—the corpse, the weight of our own unconsciousness, is resuspended, forcing him to begin all over again. This chronicity, this seemingly endless drudgery is not unlike the feeling in therapy when one is forced to confront repeatedly the same impossible dilemmas, the same dream, the same passions. The king's haulage is the same as our recognition that we do not get rid of our problems in individuation, that we do not finally "solve" or "resolve" our complexes, but rather must bear them with a different attitude so that they might reveal to us a deeper meaning. For these are stories that challenge consciousness, that force us to realize that all is not what it seems to be and that individuation is a learning process rather than an investment strategy to accrue more and more maturity points. And that we must pursue this process in the solitude of our own hearts, with bravery but not with the fantasies of power, specialness or pride, even if we feel we might burst in the process.

The stories themselves tell us much about unlived life as well. The first seems almost to parody the major elements in the king's own situation, complete with a disguised beggar ascetic. In the second, we see how even high birth does not protect one from blind possession, from the chaos of desire. The thorny issue of worldly and otherworldly lineage are the subject of the third, as is the odd kinship between thief and prince, high and low. And in the fourth, the spirit almost taunts the king by presenting him with a riddle of transposed heads, as if to force him to recognize that, contrary to what he may think, "the head ranks supreme among the members." These stories represent "all of life with its joys and horrors," the life of which the king in his infinite wisdom, was entirely unaware. Furthermore, the fact that there are twenty-four stories reiterates that we are dealing with a "lifetime," a full cycle of experience, a second chance, if you will, for the king to learn that he cannot know everything and that he must realize, in silence—as Zimmer says in his commentary on the story—that "everything is in some deep way its opposite." Thus, it is with the final riddle, about the unspeakably complex consequences of judging by misleading appearances, that the king finally wins the corpse and the admiration of the spirit. This reflective silence is the beginning of real wisdom. The king's forfeiture of needing to determine right or wrong, black or white, underscores that individuation is the apprehension of identity within diversity, of the hidden unity in the multiplicity.

At this juncture of the tale, the spirit reveals the ascetic's malevolent intent and enlightens the king as to how to defeat him. By now it is plain that king and magician are mirror images of one another, both ambitious in their own ways, both driven by power; one seemingly for good, the other certainly for ill. Yet when one is unconscious, no matter what the intent, the drive for power destroys rather than creates, inhibits freedom rather than makes way for it. Only when this drive, this desire to control life, is relinquished and when one allows oneself to be guided by the inner world can there be true freedom from perverting life through illusory rationality and self-aggrandizement. Selfishness and self-centeredness must give way to inner centeredness or wisdom.

When we are open to the unconscious, in dialogue with it, and listen to its many voices rather than command them, reflect and discern them rather than judge them, then is the domination of the head overthrown and a way made to glimpse the unity of all life. The crowning expression of this is the king's audience with Lord Shiva once he has vanquished the magician and come to know his mind and heart. Lord Shiva, the creator and destroyer, the transcendental backdrop of all life, reveals to the king that he is indeed one with all, that his victory is a universal one, for upon his individuation rides the well-being of the entire cosmos.

How are we to understand this development in psychological terms? When, in the course of the dialogue with the unconscious, and amidst the eternal differentiation of the inner world and the recognition that inner and outer are mirror reflections of one another, each filled with meaning, when we realize that the opposites of life are secretly one, then can we appreciate the immensity of our apperception, then are we able to feel connected to the larger than life within. Then do all the parts sing in harmony and with one voice. Forearmed with such experience, we may wield the sword "Invincible," the supreme tool of discernment that, like some marvelous talisman, embodies the connection that we have in real time with the timeless world within.

But where is the last aspect of individuation, its nature as process rather than goal? I see this in the king's wish, his desire that these twenty-four stories, together with the fantastic story of this eternal night, be made known all over the earth. Whosoever recites any or all of it with sincere devotion shall be free from sin. In so desiring, the king links his experience to all humanity and makes it, instead of an end in itself, an opportunity for universal redemption. Others need not literally undergo his trials to accomplish what he has accomplished, but simply know about them, become conscious of them with sincerity and with humility. Then they, too, will, as Zimmer says, move from "pompous egotism through the realm of death and finally to the summit of enlightenment." By giving the story of his journey to all people, the king in effect recognizes that there is no end point, no ownership over consciousness making or individuation and that it goes on co-eternally in all people whenever the deepest layers of life are engaged in a conscious, meaningful way. By making his tale everyone's, the king enables all selves to gather, to share in the process.

From a personal perspective this means that when we as seekers explore our lives most fully, our inner cosmos rejoices in the knowledge that ego-consciousness has joined the psyche as a whole and that a community of selves has been created. And from an outer perspective, only when we undertake this task and become free of unconscious possession and projections, can we finally see and appreciate, that is to say, gather to us, the uniqueness of others, those selves without, in reciprocal, authentic relationship.

Music of the Night: Phantoms and Relationship

MARITA DIGNEY

In the old Celtic lunar calendar, October is the last month of the year. Each day the darkness increases noticeably. The nights get longer. In a poetic sense, when is there a better time to listen to the music of the night? The days approaching the Celtic New Year, a day known as Samhain (Sow-wain), our November 1, were sacred days in which the relationship between the ancestors and the living was contemplated, celebrated and feared. The vigil of this feast, which we now celebrate as Halloween, contains folk wisdom about the nature of the human personality and relationships.

The Celtic feast celebrated the time between the end of one year and the beginning of the next. It was considered "a time between time," a sacred time when the underworld of the spirits of the ancestors had access to the upper world through this opening between the years. The upper world of everyday life also had access to the underworld. In addition to familial spirits being able to haunt their offspring at this time, the spirits of civilizations long dead were believed to have access to the descendants of their conquerors, who were the present residents of the everyday world. Some of this contact between the worlds was positive and useful; some of it was seen as gravely dangerous.

It was believed that during this time ordinary people could acquire the power of divination. For instance, a white stone placed on the embers of the bonfire at night, if gone by morning, indicated that the person who placed the stone would be gone by next Samhain. A young person eating an apple on the feast of Samhain would dream of his or her future spouse (hence the practice of bobbing for apples on Halloween). In the contact from the upper world to the underworld, the adept could ask for favors and knowledge from the spirits of the deceased.

The spirits of the underworld, like ghosts, fairies and shadowy specters, could enter uninvited into the life of the family and even into commerce and farming. The hanging skeletons and jack o' lanterns, themselves symbols of human sacrifice, were designed to frighten away these uninvited spectral guests. Some of the spirits were known to demand two thirds of the harvest of corn, two thirds of the cow's milk and two thirds of the newborn infants from the last year. Many Celtic fairy tales (that is, stories of encounters with the "Fair Ones") and legends well into the Common Era contain the motif of abductions and travel between the fairy world and the everyday world. These strange comings and goings invariably occurred at Samhain.

Samhain was a doorway between worlds and between seasons through which one entered into the holiest and darkest quadrant of the year leading to the winter solstice. As Danaan Parry, writing in *The Essene Book of Days*, puts it, "symbolically, Samhain marked the entry into the deep cavern of the Earth Mother's womb, the creative abyss, from which grows all that is intuitive and contemplative and natural on this earth." Ritual bonfires held at this time both celebrated the harvest and allowed people to burn images of the old year so they could enter the new year clean and free. These uninvited visits from the spirits of the dead were the Celtic world's version of the Hebraic concept of the sins of the fathers being visited upon the sons until the seventh generation.

What I have to say about relationship is grounded in just this kind of ancient wisdom, this kind of elemental truth. Specters and phantoms of ancestors living and dead can and do color the experience of a lifetime. Every analyst's office is littered with them, as is every life and surely every relationship. From a Jungian perspective, those intrapsychic conflicts and imbalances, which are unconscious, determine the nature and often the course of outer relationships. Unconscious identification with parental and ancestral complexes, and the unmet needs as a result of these, sap life energy every bit as much as the fairy who shows up at Samhain demanding two thirds of the corn of the recent harvest. Consider the son or daughter who is driven by an ambition which reflects the parent's unmet need for power and accomplishment, such as the phenomenon of the stage mother or the demanding Little League father. Or consider the pious minister's child who breaks the law. The survivors of refugee or concentration camps managed to cope with their repression, but their children and grandchildren may experience unmanageable depression.

In 1931, Jung wrote of this phenomenon: "What usually has the strongest psychic effect on the child is the life which the parents (and ancestors too. . .) have not lived. . . . To put it bluntly, it is that part of life which they have always shirked, probably by means of a pious lie. That sows the most virulent germs" (CW 17, par. 87). "Germs" in this instance can be understood metaphorically as a Swiss equivalent of the ancient Celtic ghosts or the Hebraic sins of the fathers.

Stories often illustrate psychological truths which cannot be fully expressed in expository speech or writing. To discuss, therefore, the multiple levels of consciousness and their impact on relatedness, I will tell an old story that presently wears a fairly modern and popular costume, the 1911 French novel *Phantom of the Opera* by Gaston Leroux.

The Andrew Lloyd Webber musical version of that novel was estimated by the *Philadelphia Inquirer* in 1993 to have sold a billion dollars in tickets worldwide. Even with five touring casts across the United States, the musical was usually sold out before it opened. After five years, *The Phantom of the Opera* remains one of Broadway's hottest tickets even though the original 1986 London cast is long gone. Since the publication of the novel in 1911, there have been three major versions—one made for television, a movie and a rock musical, *Phantom of the Paradise*, not to mention three different paperback editions of the original novel currently in book stores and an oversized glossy coffee table book with pictures and the history of each of the major productions. Cassettes and CDs of the musical have been sold to millions. A response of this magnitude tells us that something in this melodramatic, not particularly literary, part detective story, part horror story is striking a very loud chord in the contemporary psyche. Its cross-cultural appeal tells us that this story touches the deep layers of the psyche which Jung called the collective unconscious.

The novel, written in the journalistic, investigative style of the early detective story, tells of the life, abduction and disappearance of a young aspiring opera singer in Paris in the late 1800s. Christine Daae, a young Norwegian woman whose mother died when she was quite young, was raised by her father, a gifted violinist who never quite lived up to his promise. Having given up trying to make a success in conventional musical circles, he spends much of his time with Christine wandering around Scandinavia from country fair to country festival playing folk music on his violin. He is accompanied in his playing by Christine, a gifted singer. Eventually father and daughter, are taken under the protection of a generous French couple, and they go with the couple to live in Paris. Christine's father dies during her late adolescence but not without sharing with her his deeply held belief about the nature of genius and musical success. There exists, he believes, an angel of music which may come and touch a musician if that musician is very fortunate. If that visit occurs, the musician achieves the highest level of accomplishment and success. Christine asks her father if the angel of music ever touched him. He answers no, but he believes the angel may come to Christine.

As the novel opens, Christine is in the chorus of the Paris Opera company and serves as understudy for the diva, Madame Carlotta. She is a dreamy girl, not yet recovered from her father's death. She is pretty but has a distracted, unrelated attitude toward her musical studies and life in general.

The other major figure in this drama is, of course, the phantom. We learn more about him from the novel than we do in the other versions. Born with a disfigured face, he is rejected by his mother who will only talk to him when he is wearing his mask. Experiencing rejection and shame at home, he runs off with the gypsies. Exhibited as a freak in their carnivals, he also learns magic and becomes a master ventriloquist. In the novel, he is portrayed as a multitalented singer who is adept in the black arts. Naturally brilliant, he also becomes a master architect and builder. His alienation from people is so complete, however, that he never develops a conscience and serves as a ruthless confidant to those who seek to use his gifts to accomplish evil deeds. Eric—the phantom has a name—really longs to live like everyone else but his grotesque appearance keeps him from realizing this dream. After years of traveling as a freak while also carrying on a mysterious career as the architect and advisor to sultans, Eric returns to Paris and bids on work for the construction of the Paris Opera House.

The opera house is a remarkable building of seventeen stories which covers a site of nearly three acres. Seven of these stories are below street level. The basements were so huge that opera sets could be raised and lowered intact. A stable of twenty horses was kept in one area of a basement. The stage was larger than the area of the auditorium. When construction began on the massive structure, the building project required digging so deep that the engineers hit upon an underground stream. Rather than change the site they pumped out water, built the sub-basements and then allowed water to flow back into one area as a reserve for fire protection. The lake under the opera house is still there.

I add this historical note about the opera house, which inspired this tale, because it is a captivating image of the psyche. The world of the ego corresponds to the stage where we present ourselves—dressed and rehearsed—to the world. Yet the stage represents only a minuscule part of the action of an opera production, as the ego represents but a small part of the action in the psyche. The unconscious can be likened to the seven stories underground. There waiting for their part in the dramatic action are the "sets"—aspects of life and various archetypal subpersonalities.

A statue of Apollo adorns the roof of the opera house, suggesting the higher realms of human potential— light, reason and clarity. The story of the falling chandelier (which in the Andrew Lloyd Webber version of the story has the phantom riding the chandelier toward the stage) is actually based on a documented event in which part of the support of the massive chandelier fell and killed a woman attending the opera. In relating this event to the action of the phantom, the author unknowingly suggests a Luciferian quality of this dark figure as "light bearer." Christine, on the other hand, is the archetypal maiden, the Kore.

We could view this tale as primarily one of rape and abduction and ask ourselves why millions are fascinated with it. Like the story of Beauty and the Beast and the Homeric account of the abduction of Persephone by Hades (which is the archetypal source for the story we are discussing), *The Phantom of the Opera* can be interpreted sociologically. As such, this tale does comment on the culture in the sense that Marie-Louise von Franz meant when she said that the fairy tale is the culture speaking of itself. How then are we to understand the violence and sadism reflected in this story? The abduction of Persephone by Hades, a shadow side of Zeus, is a tale still to be told from the perspective of our culture, as the phenomenal success of *Phantom* suggests.

But for the purposes of this paper, put aside this sociological view and instead enter into this dramatic tale, letting its symbols play upon your psyche, particularly those of the masculine and feminine figures. Let each of these figures evoke aspects, subpersonalities if you will, of one psyche, one human personality as it attempts to grow and develop. Look at these figures as aspects of your own psyche. Rather than attempt yet another tortuous definition of what exactly is the feminine principle in the psyche of a man or a woman, let the image of the young beautiful Christine suggest characteristics and know these to be your own. If, as a woman, you have not met the Christine in men, you simply have not lived long or sensitively enough. Or as a man, if you lose sight of the Christine in the women, of any age, in your life, I suggest you look again. She is an eternal aspect of the human psyche, and she is always there. The man who can approach the Kore almost always has access to a woman's psyche.

A powerful image in the early part of the drama shows Christine with the phantom singing in her ear while she stands entranced, her hands hanging lifelessly at her sides. This is Christine as the psyche being captured by the dark, shadowy phantom. Like the maiden in Grimms' "The Maiden with No Hands," Christine is wounded by the father archetype in her encounter with life. The motif of no hands does not simply mean she cannot build bridges and fly airplanes. It means that the Christine part of the psyche cannot embrace life. She cannot seize the tools necessary for rudimentary ego development. She cannot hold what is hers. She may even have no sense of what is hers. Not only does what she needs and wants slip away from her but she has no ability to grasp it in the first place.

The phantom, who as a child was spoken to by his parents only when he wore his mask, provides a prototype of that part of the psyche which Jung called the shadow. All of those qualities which were unacceptable to our caregivers and significant others had to be relegated to the depths of our psyche. All that is uncivilized, unredeemed, primitive and undeveloped in ourselves, hidden, half-known, alluringly calling, that is what haunts us. It is "the bad" but highly charged, creative aspects of ourselves which form the great potential waiting to be loved and integrated in our psyches.

The phantom falls in love with Christine. He begins to talk to her through the walls of her dressing room. A gifted musician himself, he offers to teach her to develop her voice and to become a successful opera singer. Christine asks this disembodied voice, "Are you the Angel of Music?" He claims he is. Notice that this idea was given to her by her father—the father who never quite developed his gifts. As a result, his shadow, his unrealized ambition, his ghost, his sin is visited upon the psyche of his daughter—hence her vulnerability to this particular phantom of her own psyche. Hades as the shadow of Zeus captures once again the Persephone in yet another human soul. The original novel and the Andrew Lloyd Webber musical include a scene in which the phantom plays the violin to Christine from the grave site of her father. This is an amazing representation of the unrealized life of the parent overshadowing the psychological development of the child. It symbolizes as well the power of parental complexes in the psyche in determining behavior in the developing personality.

The phantom unmasked is the unloved, unadapted,

depth of the psyche which took all the hits, felt the rejection, suffered the abandonment inevitable in life while the ego pranced, danced and adapted as best it could as the curtain went up every day on the stage of life. Picture the unmasked face of the phantom and look into the face of your own suffering, neglected yet richly endowed, naturally talented self. If you haven't seen the aggressive, selfish, brilliant trickster in yourself or those around you, then you live in a delusion. He, like the Kore, is always there. The abduction of Christine by the phantom is a mixture of deception, seduction and violence. Set up to be deceived by her own desire, Christine wants to make the descent and move out of her dreamlike state.

The phantom ruthlessly removes the lead singer, Madame Carlotta, allowing Christine, as her understudy, to make a brilliant debut. She is awed by her own capacity, and this further attaches her to her still invisible mentor-angel. Then, in the underworld of the phantom's chambers, in the bowels of the opera house, on the far side of the underground lake, Christine encounters the monster for what he is. She finds a living, breathing person and not the angel of music, a role she had projected onto him. She unmasks him. She also begins to feel compassion for him and promises to marry him eventually.

In the novel, Christine, in a trancelike state, moves back and forth between the upper and lower worlds of the opera house. During this time, in the upper world, she is pursued by a young lover, a childhood sweetheart, Raoul, who calls to all that is alive, healthy and related in her. Eventually she tells everything to her lover and plans to run away with him at midnight, after her next performance. But just when she is ready to encounter life with the young, vigorous masculine Raoul, she is abducted by the phantom.

Learning of the abduction, Raoul follows the pair into the underworld and becomes the prisoner of the phantom. Christine promises to marry the phantom if he will release her lover, Raoul. The phantom pretends to do so and returns to Christine, unmasked, to consummate the marriage. At that moment, she feels genuine compassion for him. The phantom perceives her love for him. Their tears, falling to the ground and mingling, heal him. He knows that for the first time in his life he has experienced love without his mask. In that moment, he is released from his alienation and selfish madness. In a generosity bred of being truly loved, he then releases both Christine and Raoul.

The moment of greatest promise for individuation comes when we can face and embrace our own phantom. By encountering the phantom, in his own chamber, unmasked without projection either positive or negative, Christine is released to enter life in a fuller, more natural way.

One scene which takes place in the phantom's chamber is particularly significant. The phantom, who is completely mad at this point, forces Christine to turn one of two knobs; one knob will ignite tons of gunpowder and blow up the chamber and in fact the whole opera house. The other knob will set off a sprinkler system, which may risk flooding them but which will avoid the risk of explosion. Forced to choose blindly, she turns the knob which activates the sprinkler. The gunpowder, it seems to me, represents inflated, overwhelming, even if justified, rage. The water, on the other hand, may represent emotion, as one is said to be "flooded" with tears and emotion. Relatedness rather than anger and conflict makes all the difference and leads to awareness. It is this awareness which in turn leads to development, rather than captivity and loss. What is most important is that Christine has acted. She has used her hands. She has engaged herself in life.

The embrace of Christine and the phantom, together with her tears of compassion and his of acceptance, represent the integration of the dark creative aspects of the personality. Of this phenomenon Jung writes:

> The inner voice is the voice of a fuller life, of a wider, more comprehensive consciousness . . . . The fear that most people naturally have of the inner voice is not so childish as might be supposed. The contents that rise up and confront a limited consciousness are far from harmless. . . . What the inner voice whispers to us is generally something negative, if not actually evil. . . . The inner voice . . . makes us conscious of the evil from which the whole community is suffering, whether it be the nation or the whole human race. But it presents this evil in an individual form so that one might at first suppose it to be only an individual characteristic. The inner voice brings the evil before us in a very tempting and convincing way in order to make us succumb. If we do not partially succumb, nothing of this apparent evil enters into us, and no regeneration or healing can take place. If we succumb completely, then the contents expressed by the inner voice act as so many devils, and a catastrophe ensues. But if we can succumb only in part, and if by self assertion the ego can save itself from being completely swallowed, then it can assimilate the voice and we can realize that the evil was, after all, only a semblance of evil, but in reality a bringer of healing and illumination. (CW 17, par. 318)

Jung's statement is dramatized by Christine's embrace of the unmasked phantom within. The lyrics of the musical,

The Phantom of the Opera, put it this way:

Night-time sharpens,
heightens each sensation . . .
darkness stirs and
wakes imagination . . .
Silently the senses
abandon their defences . . .

Slowly, gently
night unfurls its splendour.
Grasp it, sense it—
tremulous and tender . . .
Turn your face away
from the garish light of day,
turn your thoughts away
from cold, unfeeling light—
and listen to
the music of the night . . .

This analysis would not be complete without a consideration of Christine's true beloved, the young, eager, vigorous Raoul. He acts differently than Christine. He evokes the hero who descends to the depths and secures the release of the feminine.

"The Music of the Night" from *The Phantom of the Opera*
music: Andrew Lloyd Webber
lyrics: Charles Hart
additional lyrics: Richard Stilgoe

If, as a man, you cannot see the heroic qualities in the women around you, then you are in for a surprise. If, as a woman, you cannot relate to the hero in the men around you, then you really don't know them at all.

Christine and Raoul represent the archetype of the couple: Sol and Luna, the royal wedding uniting the masculine and feminine within. The Kore, sweet potential, having experienced the shadowy depths, is united with the hero tried in the underworld. Theirs is not a love at first sight, but a love prepared for by differentiation, integration and the courage to be. A relationship of equals entered into, not to seek love but to bring love, entered not for love but with love. Stories ending with a happy couple are but models of the psychological development of one personality experiencing the real heart's desire, the union of opposites in the human soul. This is the task which is the prerequisite of any true experience of relationship in any form. It is the tale told a thousand times throughout history. The story which shouts the secret so difficult to hear. You are the hero. You are the damsel. You are the phantom. When these energies unite in your soul, new life is sure to manifest itself, and this new life will be less vulnerable to the claims of the underworld.

The Mystic Chords of Memory, The Better Angels of Our Nature

JAMES HOLLIS

All wars are civil wars; all neuroses are civil wars; different parts of the same whole are estranged and in conflict with each other. Abraham Lincoln, that wise and melancholic man, truly believed that our terrible war, with its one million casualties, was the vengeance of a just Jehovah for the sinful slavery of one part of the body politic by another. On March 4, 1861, with the fratricidal splits growing ever wider, Lincoln used the occasion of his first inaugural address to appeal to the shared history, the transcendent experience of the revolution, and the common fathers in Washington, Adams, Jefferson, and Franklin. His desperate search for unity concluded with an urgent summons to memory. The last two sentences of his speech are: "Though passion may have strained, it must not break, our bonds of affection. The mystic chords of memory, stretching from every battlefield and patriot grave to every living heart and hearthstone all over this broad land, will yet swell the chorus of the Union when again touched, as surely they will be, by the better angels of our nature."

In considering the large topic of relationships, I thought

to narrow my scope to that one relationship which we sustain from birth to grave, and possibly beyond—the relationship to ourselves. What follows is an essay (from the French *essayer*, to try or attempt something), best described as a meditation on relationship with oneself as both subject and object. I am convinced that the quality of outer relationship will never be any better than the level of consciousness attained through the relationship we have with ourselves. No outer relationship will ever be free of the unconscious traffic which we bring to it and which is brought to us by the other as well. Without this, relationship is rooted in unconscious factors and is perilously close to a sham that is no less alienating and wounding for being unconscious.

The problem I am addressing, the summons to self-knowledge, is as old as human consciousness and as infinite as the ocean. Indeed, we stand a better chance of knowing the ocean in its entirety than we do fathoming our own depths. As Sir Isaac Newton confessed, "I do not know what I may appear to the world, but to myself I seem to have been only like a boy playing on the seashore, and diverting myself in now and then finding a smoother pebble or a prettier shell than ordinary, whilst the great ocean of truth lay all undiscovered before me." As the poet Gerard Manley Hopkins added, "O the mind, mind has mountains; cliffs of fall / frightful, sheer, no-man-fathomed." Those who say that God never gives humans more than they can bear lie, for the world is full of persons destroyed by their own darkness. As an analyst friend of mine once said of her unconscious, "there is something in there which wants to destroy me." At the same time, we know there is something in there which wants our healing and our wholeness, and that the impulse to our healing and our purpose in life emanates from within. And it may be that the destruction the psyche sometimes seeks is that of a lesser vessel for the purpose of constructing a more ample one.

I have been drawn to Jungian thought and practice because of one fact, that it is an attitude toward self and a methodology and not an ideology. Yes, it is true that we employ arcane words like anima, archetype, complex, and others, but the whole thrust of Jungian thought is to promote a dialogue between ego and Self. As children we are at one with our instinctual truth, but with socialization we suffer the wounds of too-muchness or not-enoughness and wind up adapting ourselves to our wounds. As children, all of us were profoundly impressed with both our own vulnerability and the power of the environment. We have been thrown out of Eden, flung into the world to locate our own authentic destiny. That central, existential trauma becomes the source of our neurosis, the progressive estrangement of individuals from their instinctual truth.

What a difference it would make in the life of a person if the parent could have said to the child: "You are brought into life by nature having all you need. You have a great force, a great spirit, a great energy within you. Trust it, stay in contact with it, and it will always lead you toward what is right for you. Never hurt another person, but always be true to that great force within you, and you will never be alone and never without direction for your life." I have yet to find a person who heard or internalized such a message. The burden of Jungian therapy, thus, is to remind each person of that great truth within. By attendance upon symptom and symbol, by dream work and active imagination, we are reconciled to our own truth. When the ego accepts that it is not the source, and is "at the end of the rope," the true source responds. The mythic construct we call the Self is simply a way of incarnating, of talking about this locus of natural purpose within the person.

The central prognosticative indication of whether a person will make headway in therapy is whether he or she can internalize, that is, be strong enough to turn inward and face the forces contending in civil war therein. If the person stays locked in the blame of others, or seeks a realignment of the environment to render it more congenial, then he or she will stay stuck forever in a reflexive response to the outer world and will be tied to a false self, a maladaptive personality which compulsively repeats variants of the original response to life's trauma. Few, then, understand that Jungian therapy requires years of listening, attending, regressing before recovering a relationship to the instinctual self. Of course, most other psychologies and most modernist philosophies emphasize the importance of environment and the modification of behaviors. Jungian psychology is a kind of anachronism, for it takes its impetus from the tradition we call "essentialism," the hypothesis that there is a given nature, from which we may become estranged, but which in its healthful or wounded ways is always present and acting through history. For all the appeal of modernist psychologies and philosophies, I am obliged by the experience of practice and personal intuition to align myself with the unfashionable essentialist view.

If we are less persuaded by the essentialist arguments of Plato and Western romanticism today, still we sense in our bones the coursing of a deep truth. We are obliged to re-member, to recognize, to re-collect. As the *I Ching* described the person who "lives in the house of self-collection," so we are summoned to pull back the projections and re-collect them, internalize them, and integrate them.

Many years ago Milton Rokeach, who wrote *The Three Christs of Ypsilanti*, told me of his return to the small village of his birth in eastern Poland. There was one Jewish survivor of the Holocaust remaining. When the Nazis came through, they destroyed the local Jewish cemetery and used the gravestone fragments on roadsides and around lakes. That man chose as the work of the rest of his life to find all of those fragments and to reassemble the graveyard, not only as a memorial to his murdered friends and family, but also as a reconstruction of his own myth. If he is still living today, I imagine that man even now, with this infinite jigsaw puzzle, living out the metaphor which might have animated the stories of a Borges or a Kafka. Surely his heartbreaking work is less a memorial, however, than the reconstitution of his own sense of selfhood. The mystic chords of memory, indeed.

But what binds us to ourselves, keeps constancy, is dependable? We know that our cells are dying and regenerating; we are not the same eyes, the same hair, the same viscera, the same brain matter which we once were. We know with Heraclitus that we cannot step twice into the same stream, for not only does the stream flow on, but we are not even the same person the second time. What, then, provides the continuity? Is it the mystic chords of memory?

The surrealist poet Apollinaire observed that "memory is a hunting horn, whose sound dies out along the wind." What is remembered, what not? What is accurate, what not? The structural anthropologists tell us that all versions of a myth are true, for any mythologem or archetypal motif is polyfaceted and each version illumines another facet. So we may not casually talk about Dionysus or Aphrodite but must identify which Dionysus, which Aphrodite. As Claude Lévi-Strauss expressed it, "we do not claim to show how men think in myths, but how myths think themselves in men, and without their knowledge . . . myths think themselves among themselves." Jung adds, "a person does not make ideas; we could say that a person's ideas make the person" (CW 4, par. 769). It is apparent, then, that we serve ideas, whether we know it or not.

These mythic ideas are less ideas in the cognitive sense than emotionally charged imagos or images which we are then obliged to translate into tacit thoughts if we are ever to make them conscious. Thus, the wound of neglect or abandonment, for example, occasions a reflexive, phenomenological distrust of the world on the one hand and a diminished sense of self-worth or sense of solidity on the other. The objective fact that neither conclusion is warranted is lost before the subjective power of the primal experience.

What we call a complex is an emotionally charged image, containing a thought, even a fragmented *Weltanschauung*, which binds us to an earlier experience. The psyche is forever asking the implicit question "When have I been here before?" It activates that primal experience which immediately contaminates the reality of the present, however similar or different they seem. Each of us has large amounts of undigested psychic experience in our basement. When a situation occurs in the present which has an emotionally analogous link to that material, it activates the energy which was overwhelming to the child and floods the adult. The man who seeks to serve his wife with divorce papers after years of separation is paralyzed with fear. She evokes in him the stern, critical parent of his childhood, and he cannot be a bad boy in her eyes. The incest victim who repeatedly crosses boundaries is reflexively contaminating the present by the phenomenology of the past.

Last Fourth of July, a woman was observing the fireworks on Penn's Landing, in Philadelphia. Suddenly she suffered a panic attack and had to go home. She said of her experience, "I held the outside together, but inside I felt terror." During this same time, her ninety-three-year-old mother was dying. She felt shut out from her mother, now as always before. "Mom won't share anything with me, not even her death." In going through some of her mother's papers, she came across a clipping from 1942.

Although her mother was an American citizen, this woman had been born in Moscow. When the war began, she and her mother took a long train ride across Siberia to Tokyo where they were briefly imprisoned as enemy nationals. After a while they were released, and they sailed to Vancouver. The child recalled that their ship was bombed after it left Tokyo harbor and several were killed, though the ship continued to Canada. Her mother had always denied that such an incident ever occurred, and this woman thought she had merely remembered a movie or a bad dream.

But there, in a yellowed clipping, was the account in a Vancouver newspaper of the bombing of the *Empress of the Orient*, just as she had remembered. While she had certainly experienced fireworks before, she was in a particularly vulnerable psychological context while attending her mother's deathbed. The fireworks synchronistically summoned the energies of that event buried in her psyche, and she felt the old terror. When she confronted her mother, the woman still denied the event ever occurred, for motives unbeknownst to us. What the analysand concluded of this strange denial was, "Mother would never let me have my own reality." The outer fireworks replicated the falling bombs of long ago and far away, causing the undifferentiated material to surge forth with all its primal terror. Myth thinks us, as Lévi-Strauss would say, or the person's ideas, even those that are unconscious, make the person, as Jung would say.

All of us have had this kind of experience and have felt overwhelmed, stupid, embarrassed, by the force of a complex which seizes the ego and dominates it. Freud once described therapy as *Nacherziehung*, literally "after education" or "re-education." Since education comes from the verb "to educe" or "draw forth" from within, we can see that our therapy always obliges a drawing forth of that which already lies within, that which lives timelessly. The capacity of the person to heal and to outgrow the pernicious invasions of the past is in part owing to the enlargement and strengthening which we call adulthood. The adult can absorb the emotional charge which was overwhelming to the child, can put it into some sort of comparative experiential framework and assimilate its energy. This is why Jung said that we never really solve our problems, that is, our core wounds; we outgrow them, if we suffer them through.

In effect, the person is an assemblage of reflexive energies, charged mythologems, whose content owes most to the past and yet whose unassimilated energy is capable of dominating the present. The more these charged imagos are unconscious, the more the repetition compulsion, the more the past replicates itself. For this reason, we can see why the Greek tragedians observed that fate sets things in motion, but the responsibility for the decisions of one's life ultimately falls upon the shoulders of the individual. The *hamartia*, or wounded vision of one's self, is the refraction of childhood experience through which the adult makes the choices which bind and repeat the past.

Relationship, *relatio,* relate (to tell the story of) necessarily involves our case history. Yet our history is a fiction. A fiction is not something untrue; it is something made (from *facere*). Our case history is a thing made, an emotionally charged image, and a string of such images constitutes a narrative which relates itself, autonomously, in our dreams and in our waking life. Our case history is not objective reality, whatever that might be, but our mythic reality, with all its variations, all of which are true. We are at once abused child, unworthy friend, heroic voyager, child of our parents and our time, and still outside of time and carrier of archetypal energies. We will never know who we are any more than Newton could grasp the ocean of truth which roared beside him. And yet we cannot abandon the attempt to achieve a deeper relationship to our own myth.

We are living out our mythic imagos whether we will so or not. We are therefore obliged to take on the role of conscious mythographer if we are not to serve the fates which set such imagos in motion. Robert Calasso, in *The Marriage of Cadmus and Harmony*, expresses our dilemma:

> The mythographer lives in a permanent state of chronological vertigo, which he pretends he wants to resolve. But while on the one table he puts generations and dynasties in order, like some old butler who knows the family history better than his masters . . . you can be sure that on

> another table the muddle is getting worse and the threads ever more entangled. No mythographer has ever managed to put his material together in a consistent sequence, yet all set out to impose order. In this, they have been faithful to the myth . . . [for] myth allows of no system.*

Thus the mythographer knows what the therapist knows, that there is no one truth, that all the variants, even those that are contradictory, are somehow true.

This vertiginous dilemma leads us to confusion and contradiction, and yet we must continue to seek self-knowledge lest we be prisoners of our ignorance and of our fated wounds. Thus, structuralism, post-structuralism, and deconstructionism pass through as momentary philosophical and psychological fashions, each undermining the notion that there may be such a thing as truth, or an Archimedean point on which to stand or from which even to survey the terrain. We know that the primary folly imbedded in neurosis is the delusion of the ego that it is in charge, even as its suzerain is undermined by split-off contents. And it is the folly of psychosis to abandon the ego's precarious position and surrender to the command of the dark gods. Paradoxically, the reason why we pay attention to dreams, for example, is to deconstruct the false reality of conscious life and to enlarge its perspective, to see the world as that fictive construct, the Self, sees it. What is left to us, in the Jungian, post-Kantian world, is to employ our fictions as consciously as possible. We are impelled to render our mythic motifs more consciously, yes, but with the added knowledge

*Roberto Callaso, *The Marriage of Cadmus and Harmony* (New York: Alfred A. Knopf), 1993, p. 281.

that all of the variants have a truth, of sorts, and that we juggle fictions even when we talk of ego and Self, and even of the "I" who expresses these thoughts. Wallace Stevens noted this necessary, fictive shift in a poem entitled "A High-Toned Old Christian Woman." He suggests that he, the poet, and she, the theolog, are about the same thing—the making of fictions. But the poet remains free in the conscious play of fictions, while the theolog is trapped in her idolatrous literalism of certainty. He concludes, "This will make widows wince. But fictive things / Wink as they will. Wink most when widows wince." If we are to chart our own myth, in all its velleities and variants, we are obliged to wink frequently, to play with the sundry disguises of Self, lest we fall into the idolatry of literalism, the psychosis of fundamentalism.

By now we are in more than a bit of a muddle, or, as Yeats wrote, "we are locked in / and the key is turned on our uncertainty." As the neo-Kantians would have it, we can never know the *Ding-an-Sich* with ourselves as both *Ding* and the *Sich*. As Jung would have it, the damnable definition of the unconscious is that it is unconscious. As the structuralists would have it, each imago contains its opposite and, though the mind demands resolution, all variants are true. As the deconstructionists would have it, no signifier, no signified—all is context, context is all. We are well painted into a corner, then. If you are perplexed, then I have been successful. If it is true that our relationships with others can never be more conscious, or more evolved, than our relationship to ourselves, and if it is true that we do not stand a prayer of ever knowing ourselves, then relationship is either impossible or fatally impaired.

Certainly most relationships are fatally impaired, whether they be between parent and child, between social groups, or between intimate partners. And we all know ourselves to be our own worst enemies. With Oedipus we must admit that Apollo set this fate upon us, but the hand which wounded us was our own. With all this realism, this cynicism, this pessimism, we are still stunned by our secret confession, that we believe still that there is a truth deep within which we may trust if we can hold to it and bring courage to bear in order to live it. From the metaphysical and epistemological debris of modern philosophy and psychology we are still obliged to make axiological judgments. That is, without a reality ground upon which to stand, without a reliable discernment between sanity and madness, we are still obliged to make decisions and be persons of value. Such valorization of this fallen world occurs even in Sandra Bernhard's book, *Love, Love, and Love,* when she says, "Love is the only shocking act left on the face of the earth." Surveying the madness of private lives and collective politics, she notes that, nonetheless, "in the quietest night with whispers of tenderness and trust penetrating the senses, control, power, anger are thrown aside and we bear witness to the only valid instant in the universe, love."

Her invocation of love is not sentimental, nor is it escapist. It is a miraculous survivor of the civil war which has continued for millennia. Amid the savannahs of the soul, the weary and battered heart still springs anew to the summons to life. Each of us has questions still to ask and to answer in very private ways. What is your life's vocation? When did your childhood end? When did you really leave home? Have you really left home? Where are you stuck in your life? What is the unlived life which haunts you? What, on the invisible plane, supports you on the visible plane? These questions are ineluctable, inescapable, and if we do not address them consciously, our lives are still to be lived daily, but with a far greater burden of sadness, of pathos, of heaviness. This Saturnian weight derives, of course, from the soul's distress, or so we intuit.

Thus we are painted into the corner—obliged to live more consciously lest we collude and compound that wounding which fate has already given, and yet knowing no ground on which to plant the ego's flag, no rich West Indies of the soul to claim for the Old World sovereign.

Let us return to the Great Emancipator for a moment. If ever there was a large-souled person who lived with humor and sorrow in the real world, communed with noble ideas yet split rails, buried his son, sent men off to die, it was Lincoln. He had to carry his soul's heaviness, as we all do, and live in the world of daily duty, as we all do. What, then, is this talk of angels, "the better angels of our nature," which might yet unify a sundered soul and a divided land? We all know his appeal was unsuccessful. Soon the nation, North and South, was to sing, "Many are the hearts which are weary tonight / tenting on the old camp ground." Yet his appeal was correct and represents an idea which may yet save us.

In this simple sentence there are critical words which command our closer scrutiny. We recall that the medieval philosophers made much of *natura naturata* and *natura naturans*, nature natured and nature naturing. It is at the heart of the essentialist leap of faith that there is a given nature which is naturing through us whether we are conscious of it or not. Nature has a largeness of purpose, and it expresses its volitions through affective invasions, through somatic symptoms, and through the dreams which trouble sleep. But we must also note that modest word *our*, for it is our nature which we are experiencing, incarnating. Surely we will find greater courage to live out our individuation when we recall that never before in history has there been such a concatenation of atoms, such a qualitative capacity for consciousness as you represent, and never again shall such appear. So great the summons, then, to be yourself, to serve the exfoliation of your nature so that you might serve Nature itself, and others around you who depend on you to become yourself, the person to whom they are wont to relate.

But the notion of angels strikes us as quaint, even superstitious; however, we recall that angel comes from the Greek *angelos* or "messenger." We are flooded with messengers, perhaps all too many of them. Yet such visitations are precisely that which we require to navigate the perilous rapids of our journey. In his 1939 speech called "The Symbolic Life," Jung commented that we moderns have forgotten what our ancestors knew, that the silence is not silent, that the dark is luminous for those who wait upon it. When we attend the silence, wait upon the darkness, which is what the word *therapeuein* or "therapy" means, we find a wondrous luminosity and a presence which means that we are never wholly alone. To attend the better angels of our nature is to open to the possibility of healing the civil split within.

The dilemma of the modern is clear; we are painted into a corner from which there is no escape, only sticky situations. The sum of philosophical and psychological thinking over the last few centuries has ruled out the possibility of absolute or even objective knowledge. Thus, we are all in the predicament of Abraham. A voice tells us to slay our child, or slay something we have cherished from our past. Is this the voice of God, or a madness, a split-off part which possesses us? How may we ever know? Yet we are obliged to live concretely in this world, daily, and hopefully as persons of value. If there is no metaphysical Greenwich of the soul, how can we find the mythic referents which give us locus? What longitudes and latitudes may be discerned? That great sea-traveler Newton could use reason and observation as his sextant and astrolabe. We suspect that even these tools may be deceptive. And we find ourselves adrift, caught in the mythic wash and reflux of isolation and uncertainty.

Perhaps the only gambit left available to those who have painted themselves into metaphysical corners is to see the world, in the Hindu metaphor, as "God's play." If we are obliged to play the game without absolute knowledge, if winning and losing are illusions, then surely the purpose of the game is play itself. Then, if our nervous ego can stand the ambiguity, the tension of opposites, the mystery of the messengers may be celebrated. As Helen Luke wrote of our desire to hasten the end of our suffering, "you shouldn't fight a neurosis in order to get rid of it. It is probably the one thing that is necessary for you to learn what is the matter. It is, therefore, the gift of God." Similarly, Gurdjieff asked that we "remember, you've come here having already understood the necessity of struggling with yourself—only with yourself. Therefore, thank everyone who gives you the opportunity."

My intention in this essay is heuristic, to stir thought, perhaps a complex or two, and to recover a sense of mystery. While we seek clarity, we are perhaps better served to return to the solitude of our lives with a restored sense of that large ocean which roared beside Newton and which courses through our veins. If we are obliged to live without absolute knowledge, then perhaps we may find the courage to sustain, perhaps celebrate, perhaps even enjoy that ambiguity. Accordingly, rather than say, then, "I am this content, this construct, this ideology," we can say, "I am my journey." Or, "I am my dialogue with the angels, the messengers of my mystery."

The Great Emancipator sensed somehow that all wars are civil wars, that what we have not assimilated within contaminates the outer world. We can never have a viable relationship with an Other out there until we have a more evolved relationship with the Other in here. We serve relationship with others best, and participate in society best, when we attend to the unassimilated messengers of nature within each of us. Jung warned us that what is denied inwardly will come to us as outer fate. Every time we flee the Antietam of private angst, the Gettysburg of private guilt, the Fredricksburg of private fear, those aversions are revisited upon the world around us. We can only heal the world around us by healing the civil war within us. Even today, Lincoln's summons remains to stir the mystic chords of memory and attend the better angels of our nature.

The Politics of Consciousness: Individuation & "Communitation" in Human Relationships

ALDEN JOSEY

The close linking of personal and collective dynamics in the creation of consciousness is insufficiently appreciated by the world at large and, more to the point of this essay, by the Jungian community. In our collective, public life, we get into unattractive, discouraging and destructive displays of unconsciousness at work. We are perhaps no worse in this regard than other collectives, say, for example, the United States Senate, but it is rather perplexing that a community dedicated to the study and advancement of the Jungian model of psychodynamics should be so vulnerable to the dark energies in the unconscious collective that it has done so much to explain.

Or perhaps it is not at all so perplexing, if (and this would please Jung) we can claim, through our studies and through personal analytic work, some sense of the perverse doings of the shadow and that we understand very well how the shadow infiltrates human intercourse, especially ours, and causes trouble. What distinguishes Jungian communities is that we have a deep respect for the psychic energies locked in such dark unconscious spaces, and we have a genuine wish to rescue these energies for the purposes of conscious individual and group life. Jung made this very clear when he said:

> The conscious achievement of inner unity clings desperately to human relationships as to an indispensable condition, for without the conscious acknowledgment and acceptance of our kinship with those around us there can be no synthesis of personality . . . . The inner consolidation of the individual is not just the hardness of collective man on a higher plane, in the form of spiritual aloofness and inaccessibility; it emphatically includes our fellow man. (CW 16, par. 444)

These comments are direct and unmistakable; Jung thought that individuation is only half the story. In actual fact, it is a profound misunderstanding of the processes of psychological development not to see that the newly won ground of personal consciousness has the deepest implications for the transformation of relationships at every level.

This means for me that individuation, as a central obligatory task of every person to incarnate his or her own uniqueness, is ultimately in some measure a political act So I refer to the politics of individuation, to the politics of the creation of consciousness, with every intended reference to the Greek root word πολιτψ (*politeia*), which connotes ideas of "citizenship, life of a citizen, fellow citizen, government, democracy, commonwealth." I want to emphasize the dynamism that links the fate of individuals with that of the collective for good or for ill.

In "The Psychology of the Transference," Jung gives us a marvelous start toward understanding the pyschodynamics of relationship in a model developed for his study of some alchemical pictures in their connection to transference. The suggestive power of Jung's model is extraordinary and reaches beyond the relatively limited use that he made of it in examining the unconscious features of relationship. This is where I shall begin in order to get a deeper understanding of the politics of consciousness.

Every human relationship has an *intra*psychic and an *inter*psychic component and each component has a conscious and an unconscious part. This is true not only in dyadic but also in group relationships and introduces factors that only grow more complex as the size of the group increases. The folk wisdom that "two's company, three's a crowd!" recognizes that the relationship of A and B is complicated by the arrival of C, which adds to the original problems the new ones of the relationships of A and B to C.

The intrapsychic component includes the interactions between the personal conscious and the personal and collective unconscious. These interactions occur especially in the striving of an individual to come to terms with his or her own psychological potential and to bring that potential into conscious reality. This is a matter of a relationship to oneself and is, of course, the basis of the process that Jung called individuation.

If you fulfill the pattern that is peculiar to yourself, you have loved yourself, you have accumulated, you have abundance; you bestow virtue then because you have luster, you radiate, from your abundance something overflows. But if you hate yourself, if you have not accepted your pattern, then there are hungry animals, prowling cats and other beasts in your constitution which get at your neighbors like flies in order to satisfy the appetites which you have failed to satisfy (*Nietzsche's* Zarathustra, part 6, lecture 2).

The interpsychic component is the relationship with other people; it is the zone of our encounter with the collective in all its forms, from the collective of two in the most intimate connections of our lives to the larger collectives of family, tribe, nation and species. Within this zone are all the struggles that individuals go through, in a group context, to lift their discourse out of the dark, undifferentiated strata of unconscious, moblike interactions into the light of conscious self-and-other awareness. I call this process *communitation.* It is the archetypal complement of the energies that go to create the individual into his or her own uniqueness. Communitation emphasizes not only the necessity and the value of the coalescence of individuals into communities, but also the processes through which the collective conscious becomes stronger, more coherent and more humane.

These two complementary aspects of psychic life are indissolubly linked in a polarity that lives and breathes in a constant systole and diastole, a dance of psychic energy, if you will, in which we are all perforce participants whether through our conscious willing or through the autonomous dynamism of the unconscious complexes.

In making the distinction between individuation and individualism, Jung made it clear how the latter, so highly prized as a virtue in contemporary Western society, is destructive of communitation.

> Individualism means deliberately stressing and giving prominence to some supposed peculiarity rather than to collective considerations and obligations. But individuation means precisely the better and more complete fulfillment of the collective qualities of the human being . . . . Individuation, therefore, can only mean a process of psychological development that fulfills the individual qualities given; in other words, it is a process by which a man becomes the definite, unique being he in fact is . . . . The individualistic emphasis on one's own peculiarity is a contradiction of this basic fact of the living being (a living unit, composed of universal factors, wholly collective). Individuation, on the other hand, aims at a living cooperation of all factors. (CW 7, par. 267-269)

When, for example, within a Jungian community we experience these seismic events, and particularly after their shock has faded, we want to understand how we have "been had" and what to do about it, so that our communitation process lifts to a new level before the next inevitable event. These experiences, in their nature, are political in the classical sense, that is, they are products of a clash of interests within a group. We may, therefore, properly speak of the dynamics of the psychological development of collectives as the politics of consciousness.

Jung's original model expresses the empirical fact that in any paired relationship there is a pattern of flow of psychic energy in which conscious and unconscious influences are exchanged between the partners. It identifies six pathways or axes of exchange, which taken together constitute the archetypal field of the total interaction, including its intrapsychic and interpsychic aspects.

As individuals are unique, so their combinations are unique. Thus each human relationship modeled in this way will produce a unique pattern of the flow of psychic energy.

This pattern is itself a unique reality of varying intensity, a kind of "third thing," which exists in the psychological field of the relationship.

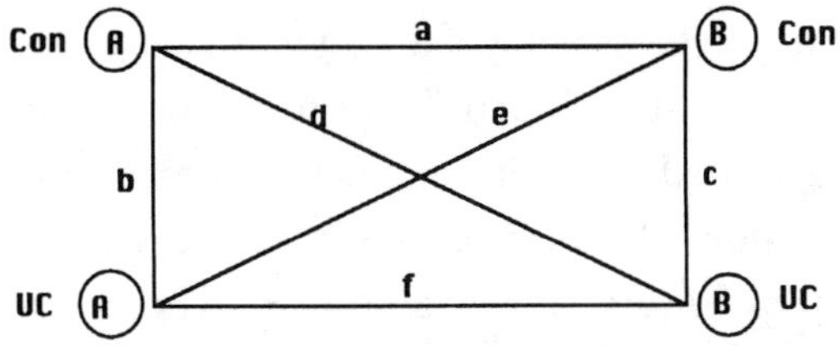

Fig. 1

An Interactional Model for Relationship of A and B

In the model for the relationship of two individuals (figure 1), line (a) is the axis of conscious communication of the pair A and B, who may be, for instance, analyst and analysand, husband and wife, teacher and student, employer and employee or any other of a host of dyadic interactions. The vertical line (b) represents the intrapsychic axis in A which expresses the interactions between conscious and unconscious aspects of that personality, and line (c) denotes the corresponding contents of B. The diagonals (d) and (e) represent the process through which unconscious contents of B and A, respectively, are projected onto the partner. Projection is a universal process in relationships by which either negative or positive contents, neither of which is conscious, are expelled into others and experienced as belonging to the other rather than to oneself.

Line (f) represents communication that takes place between two persons without either one being conscious of the exchange. In fact, the dynamics of a relationship may be dominated by such unconscious exchanges, as noted below in the example of a married couple.This is the axis that comprises the participation mystique, a state of symbiotic identity or fusion and of projective identification.

In projective identification, as Robert Langs has said, "I evoke in you something of my own inner state so that you will experience it and identify with me. But in addition, I remain identified with whatever I am projecting onto you in the interaction." It takes place when split-off parts of the personality of A are "injected" into B, who is particularly disposed to accept and identify with the projected contents. For example, a man whose need for intimacy and closeness is highly split off and unconscious "delegates" that role to his wife, who, in turn, is unconscious of her own needs for space and solitude, which are "delegated" to her husband. Each has failed to make a conscious contact with and integrate a range of emotional needs that include both intimacy and distance.

This couple has made an unconscious arrangement to live as "part-personalities" and to realize these needs in the relationship; that is, the psychological work that each needs to do in the intrapsychic field has been projected into the interpsychic field, and the necessary personality developments do not occur. He withdraws from intimacy and seeks privacy (while secretly needing her to press closer to him), while she tries to create as much shared space as possible (while secretly needing him to establish some distance for her).

Projective identification works in this way to create unconscious dependence, along with its nagging discontents, between the partners. Each needs the other to bear and to enact denied parts of themselves. The psyche suffers the loss that arises from the failure of each person to live his or her own life in a conscious way. When the Self generates internal needs for development in dependent personalities caught in these kinds of unconscious entanglements, it can cause a full range of neurotic symptoms which express impulses to make the shadow conscious and to integrate it into life.

These dynamics are at work not only in dyadic relationships but also in the interactions of larger collectives. I have expanded, in figure 2, the original model to consider interactions among a group of seven persons, indicated by a hexagonal array of figures around a central figure, on which we focus our attention in a kind of "freeze frame" view. Again, the top layer represents conscious interaction and the bottom layer unconscious interaction. Even larger collectives may be constructed by extending the interactions of the peripheral figures to other individuals in an ever-expanding network of interrelationship.

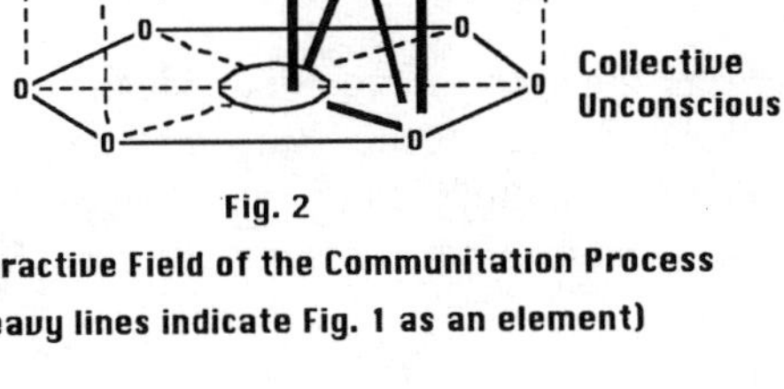

Fig. 2
The Interactive Field of the Communitation Process
(Heavy lines indicate Fig. 1 as an element)

The portion of the figure drawn with heavy lines is identical with the earlier model showing how the dyadic interaction is a kind of structural element in what is now a vastly more complex web of psychic interaction. Some of the paths of interaction between the central figure and the others are drawn, but most are omitted for clarity. All the figures are related with varying intensity of exchange with all other figures in this model.

How is such a picture useful in understanding the psychodynamic of collectives? We can see that just as there is a network of conscious interaction among the group, there is also a nexus of unconscious content, an expandable reservoir of personal and collective unconscious factors. These may now begin to interact with each individual as a mass of undifferentiated but potent energy which can reach a stage of critical mass with the power of a strong gravitational pull on single persons.

Out of such dynamics mobs are formed with the power to absorb otherwise independent persons and subvert their psychic independence to the collective unconsciousness of the herd. These processes are effective at the level of the street as well as in the affairs of nations, as the sorrowful history of the twentieth century shows. Jung writes:

> The greater the aggregation of individuals, the more the individual factors are blotted out, and with them morality, which rests entirely on the moral sense of the individual and the freedom necessary for this. (CW 7, par. 240)

Since I have already mentioned the U.S. Senate, it is helpful to recall what the Romans said about their own senate: *Senatus bestia, senatores boni viri.* Jung's comment, something of a paraphrase, was "the bigger the organization, the more unavoidable is its immorality and blind stupidity," and further on he says, "any large company composed of wholly admirable persons has the morality and intelligence of an unwieldy, stupid and violent animal" (CW 7, par. 240).

In smaller collectives where the members may be relatively well acquainted with each other, psychic infection can arise from an individual in whom unconscious contents of a personal and an archetypal nature are particularly strongly constellated. In this kind of situation, highly autonomous, unconscious factors activated in a particular individual strike powerful resonances in other susceptible members of the group, especially when the contents are archetypal in nature and when the conscious personalities are not stable enough to resist the infectious agent. The Salem witch hysteria is a classic case of this kind. There are many contemporary examples, such as the case in the former Yugoslavia where villagers who had lived in relative peace for years turned on each other in a fury of murderous passion rooted in religious and ethnic differences.

Again, if an individual of particular power or influence or intelligence, that is to say, a charismatic person, in a collective experiences the irruption of unconscious contents in such a way as to constitute a temporary madness, it is not uncommon for that person through his or her charisma to amplify a largely personal episode into a compelling action or movement that sweeps up others by its sheer iridescent attractiveness. The inflation that goes along with such temporary possessions brings with it a certain "godliness," a kind of universal validity, that always accompanies identification with the collective psyche.

Here the subjective mental space of an individual is

transformed into an objective fact, such as a popular religious or political cause, that acts like a field of gravity upon nearby members of the community to draw them as willing satellites. Examples of this phenomenon abound among the founders of religious sects and secular utopian communities, political dissidents who parlay personal disaffections into concentrations of power large and small, and others who contrive to play out in public what are, or might better be, largely private and personal dramas. These are the times when one's own "hungry animals, prowling cats and other beasts," rather than being kept in an inner zoo, are unleashed upon one's neighbors.

In the Jungian community there is a certain split, a kind of disjointed quality in our groups and societies which hinders the development of a critical mass of collective consciousness, our main protection against epidemics of psychic infection. There are, for example, the conflicts that sometimes arise between advocates of either "classical" or "revisionist" approaches to Jung's writings. There are also conflicts regarding the personal history of Jung himself. Strong emotions are constellated, and feelings of mistrust and estrangement arise that interfere with practical aspects of community life, such as the organization of programs, lectures and the like. Projections fly like arrows between warring camps, and the power of mutually unconscious factors to ensnare people of thoughtful good will cannot be underestimated.

Projective identification is also often at work, and, in a case like that described above, it is not unlikely that the "classicists" harbor unconscious doubts and concerns about Jung and all his works. In turn, the "revisionists" may well long for a strong, loving, and steady figure to anchor them against conscious tendencies to disrupt and rearrange. Each group is caught in an unconscious tide in which the other is asked, even coerced, to enact its own secret needs.

These destructive dynamics have been known to complicate relationships between Jungian institutes. Partisan feelings divide groups into factions over programs, policies and training methods. One hears the complaints "not symbolic enough!" or "not clinical enough!" as if a truly contemporary and effective institute does not need to embody both in appropriate measure in the service of the individual and communitation processes. I don't doubt that what is at work here, as well as in the more local imbroglios, is a mass of poorly understood and insufficiently resolved unconscious factors.

These episodes, ranging from comic to tragic in scope, often have an aftermath. In this period, when the infection has subsided, it is not uncommon for persons to ask "What happened to me, to us? How did I, we, ever get drawn into that?" This is that moment when a temporarily displaced consciousness reestablishes itself, often shakily, and looks around to check the damage. It is at such moments when the politics of individuation/communitation become crucial elements of community life, when the search begins for new ways to shore up the shared system of conscious values.

An essential prophylactic against such psychic infections, epidemics of unconsciousness with potential for crushing the life of the spirit in individuals and communities, is the building of institutions that protect and nurture the conscious levels of all relationships. We need to consider some way to ensure the mediation of disputes or discord that affect the life of the community as a whole. Were such institutions for the fostering of collective consciousness present in some of the pathological situations we get ourselves into, at least on the small scales, it is possible that many destructive outcomes would be avoided or, at least, their impact lessened. Keeping in mind the community diagram, it is vital that where epicenters of unconscious infection flare, there should be something like a community "immune response" that absorbs the event and prevents a spreading of destructive unconscious energies.

Traditionally, personal contacts, often carried out sub rosa, have sufficed to forestall serious trouble; somebody talks to somebody. But this approach ignores the need for psycho-political institutions, forms that go beyond the purely personal to concentrate and affirm collective conscious values against attacks from unconscious factors. In traditional societies like those of Native Americans, councils of wise men and women have acted as guardians of collective consciousness, reconciling differences and making peace. Is this a clue for us? Perhaps it is time for the Jungian community to make the effort to create such institutions.

Yet, it is paradoxically in the personal sphere, in the intrapsychic work of individuation that the groundwork is laid for all higher forms of collective conscious life. It is psychologically sound to claim that in all relationships, but especially in the relationship of two, which is the simplest community, the most effective way to transform the interpersonal field is to do one's own personal work. It is deeply true that we cannot cast the mote out of the other's eye.

The psychology of Jung affirms this truth as one of its most central assertions.

Whatever institutions communities develop to safeguard their psychic health, they will all rest upon the psychological maturity, the conscious self-knowledge of the individual person. It is this atom of personal consciousness that is the basic building block the fate of which is to create healthy human collectives. Those who adhere to the critical propositions of a humanist psychology must test their survivability in the real world of human encounters and struggles. This is what makes individuation, ultimately, a political matter.

Wild Analysis: Apollo and Cassandra

Alexander McCurdy III

Although the analytic relationship is not a paradigm for relationship in general, what I have to say about "wild analysis" can apply to personal relationships whether in friendship, in marriage or in the family. Basic psychoanalytical concepts are familiar to many persons today. Even a high school student can understand how defense mechanisms, such as denial or projection, function in hiding unconscious processes. These psychological concepts, however, are not just benign ideas; they are tools which provide a crude kind of leverage, and therefore power, to anyone who decides to use them. An analogy could be made to the high-powered pneumatic drills used by dentists today. Conceivably, anyone could pick up that drill and make a tooth disappear in a matter of minutes, but we can imagine the results when we know that even a well-trained professional has to be extremely careful when using it. Psychoanalytic insights, too, are powerful tools which can be misused in private relationships, just as they can be misused in the professional relationship when the analyst does not pay very close attention to the situation at hand.

Although to my knowledge Jung never used the expression "wild analysis" (a term coined by Freud), he wrote vehemently on the subject from the perspective of the archetypal dimensions in the relationship between the ego and the unconscious. My argument is that "wild analysis" continues to be a problem. It is not an outdated topic, and it is, I would argue, as pertinent to this generation as it was to Freud's and Jung's.

By "wild analysis" Freud meant the imparting of psychoanalytic interpretations to individuals not psychologically prepared to hear or comprehend them. Wild analysis occurs when an individual's psychological material is interpreted by someone who is insufficiently trained in psychoanalytic theory and practice. In the article "Concerning 'Wild' Psychoanalysis" (1910), Freud takes up the matter of a physician who, having studied Freud's theories, interpreted the anxieties of a woman patient. When asked to speak to this woman, Freud found her far more distraught and anxious after being subjected to the doctor's "wild" interpretations than before. He points out several problems with the physician's work.

The case concerned a woman in her late forties suffering from anxiety states precipitated, as Freud tells us, by her recent divorce. Matters got much worse, however, after she had visited her doctor, who informed her that her anxiety was related to the accumulation in her of sexual energies and desires. She would be cured, he insisted, if she would do one of three things: return to her husband, take a lover, or learn to satisfy herself by masturbation.

Freud's thoughts on the case are quite interesting in themselves, but apart from the physician's misunderstanding of the psychological material in the first place, he points out the technical errors which were made. Freud says,

> It is a long superseded idea, and one derived from superficial appearances, that the patient suffers from a sort of ignorance, and that if one removes this ignorance by giving him information . . . he is bound to recover. The pathological factor is not . . . [a patient's] ignorance in itself, but the root of this ignorance in . . . inner resistances; it was they that first called this ignorance into being, and they still maintain it now. (SE XI, p. 225)*

In wild analysis resistances are ignored. Instead, in an attempt to help by providing information, clients are given the naked truth. For example, persons suffering from agoraphobia are told that they have dangerously expansive tendencies and are thereby confronted point-blank with internal psychological contents that they are unconsciously projecting onto the world outside the doors of their house. Most likely, this will cause anger, anxiety or resistance, and reactions in the patient that will not help at all. What is totally neglected in attempting this type of wild analysis is that the reason a projection of unconscious contents occurs in the first place is that the contents are too frightening to allow into consciousness. Direct confrontation with such a defense simply stirs up problems and doesn't solve them. A similar situation occurs when a wife repeatedly tells her alcoholic husband that he is denying his drinking problem. She, too, will meet with little success and probably stir up even more denial and trouble in attempting this particular brand of domestic wild analysis.

How easy it is to forget that psychological disturbances, as treated in the depth psychology of both Freud and Jung,

---

* *The Standard Edition of the Complete Works of Sigmund Freud* (London: The Hogarth Press, 1963).

are not based on ignorance, but on unconscious blocks in the mind. Freud called these blocks "defenses" or "resistances." Jung did too, but added that these blocks were based on the natural inhibition of an immature ego. Behind the defenses lie the unconscious contents. Often both the blocks and the contents being blocked are unconscious. For example, the defense (denial) of alcoholics is usually unconscious. They think they are telling the truth when they are actually denying it. In addition to their unconsciousness about the defense, alcoholics are usually quite unaware of the unconscious contents, often depressive elements, against which they are defending themselves in the first place. We are talking about a double unconsciousness here. Enter the well-intentioned person armed with the interpretive tools of depth psychology, which grant even a beginner the power to see and understand things that are totally unconscious to another person. Such facile knowledge leads quickly to a temptation to inform someone exactly how they are "rationalizing," "projecting," "denying" and so on. Wishing to help, the beginner is sometimes greatly tempted to do this. However, subtle power motivations can also arise, feeding the desire to lord it over another person with one's newly acquired psychological "truth." In either instance, it is far more harm than good that is usually done.

The interpretive tools of psychoanalysis, which Jung never discarded even after he split from Freud, are, in fact, powerful. The insight they provide can tempt us to try to help people overcome blocks by simply giving them information and interpretations about their psychological condition. They are told what they are blocking, not how and why. Many of us, after learning a little about psychoanalysis, have felt this same temptation. To know even a little about the unconscious, about how it works, about its defensive and its prospective functions, can give us an irresistible sense of power. Suppose, for example, that you see quite clearly that a person is unconscious of projecting. It might be the case of someone who is very passive-aggressive accusing another person, irritated about a small event, of being an aggressive monster. How tempting it is for us to want to tell the pot, who is calling the kettle black, just how black the pot itself is.

To give another example: Freud described what he called a "reaction formation," in which a person substitutes feelings of one sort for feelings of exactly the opposite kind. A man, for instance, will consciously show affection for another person when, in fact, unconsciously he harbors angry or even hateful feelings toward that person. The observer with the powerful interpretive tools of psychoanalytic understanding may see clearly what is happening, although the man in question cannot.

We are talking here about the issue of power. Psychoanalytic insight, which enables us to recognize something that is going on in others that they themselves cannot see, also gives us considerable power over them. And, let me stress, this power, in its rawest form, is easy to attain. All we need to do is read and study some basic analytic texts, attend some lectures, and observe people. More difficult, however, is the ability to understand and judiciously apply the power, channeling it into productive, rather than destructive ends.

Freud points to two problems which are at the root of wild analysis: first, the doctor did not understand psychoanalytic theory sufficiently, and second, he made technical errors in the application of those aspects of the theory which had been understood—chiefly, by not adequately considering the psychological resistances or immaturity of the patient. In the case described by Freud there may have been some truth in the explanations the doctor gave his patient, but by giving the patient only partially true interpretations, without understanding the patient's psychology, he only made matters worse.

Both problems can be corrected by deeper knowledge and more training. Freud's response to this problem was the formation in 1910 of the International Psycho-Analytical Association. Jung, who was collaborating closely with Freud at this time, became its first president. The members of this association were trained in the field of psychoanalysis.

In the years preceding the publication of the article on wild analysis, Freud and Jung had lengthy discussions about the problems pertaining to the practice of analysis in general and about problems of wild analysis. Initially, Jung had suggested to Freud that in addition to the lack of theoretical knowledge and technical skills, there was also a third factor—the doctor's own lack of adequate psychological development. At issue was the doctor's connectedness to, and awareness of, his/her own unconscious and the need to attend to the propensity to project unconscious material in dealing with patients. Jung was emphasizing that the analyst is a major healing factor in the analytic process.

But Jung's attitude of scientific openness in stressing the importance of the practitioner's personality should not be confused with the compromising of certain fundamentals about the practice of depth psychology. The following principles always remained basic for Jung: first, that a practitioner know the theoretical material; second, that a practitioner know the methods of dealing with this material when consulting with a client, and third, that a practitioner be analyzed, preferably by one or more persons well trained in preparing candidates for the pitfalls and difficulties of doing analytic work. Because the analyst's personality is so important in the analytic process, highly developed skills are called for, particularly with regard to transference, which proved to be extremely tricky to monitor successfully.

The necessity to train future analysts vied with Jung's conscious distaste for the idea of creating "Jungians" as clones of himself. No doubt this was in part a reaction to his personal experience with Freud and to having been a witness to the making of "Freudians," whose fidelity to the master's discoveries seemed so one-sided. This distaste for creating "Jungians" may have been a shadow aspect of the intensity with which Jung so confidently knew what he knew, leading to a conscious expectation that others should see things his [Jungian] way also.

Like Freud, Jung espoused experiment and new insights, but well bounded by due respect for an analytic method that would not discard basic principles. Like Freud, Jung himself analyzed and trained the first candidates in these principles. He also decided when he thought they were ready. But with increasing numbers of candidates coming to be trained, Jung could no longer handle the training himself. And so was founded the C. G. Jung Institute in Zürich and, eventually, the International Association of Analytical Psychology with its associated training institutes around the world.

No one would argue that Jung was right in all his judgments or scientific opinions. Nor are all those trained in his analytic method right at all times in their judgments. From time to time mistakes are made with wild analysis. The point is that wild analysis is less likely to occur among those who have been adequately analyzed and well schooled in both the theory and the practice. The fundamental principles learned in the training serve as reference points by which wild analysis can be both defined and successfully avoided.

As Jung's research into the archetypal dimensions of the psyche deepened, his warnings about the Jungian equivalent of wild analysis increased. This is most clearly seen in his article "The Relations Between the Ego and the Unconscious," first published in 1916 and, because of its importance, revised and reworked many times by Jung. One of the issues Jung stresses in it concerns the dangers and pitfalls that the ego faces when assimilating aspects of the unconscious. Although Jung is speaking of someone confronting his/her own unconscious, what he describes applies equally to a person who is delving into someone else's psychological material.

The potential misuses of psychoanalytic power become even more significant when we consider the levels of the psyche that Jung opened up for us in his researches and writings. The power of Jung's insights is even more impressive and potentially more dangerous than Freud's. Freudian wild analysis pales next to Jungian wild analysis. Someone's archetypal dreams, for example, may stir up in the person looking at the material ideas, feelings and wishes which need to be controlled. This can be the case whether it be a professional analyst at work or an ordinary person with a friend. It may be that admiration or awe are awakened along with an urgent wish to interpret or to amplify what has been revealed about that someone's psyche. The unconscious is seductive; its ambivalences, which may be poisonous or curative, can incite the naive or self-anointed practitioner into wild interventions into another's process. In certain instances, this same seductiveness of the unconscious can deceive the naive into being silent, shrouding the fact that the time is ripe for a necessary intervention. No word of warning is spoken when it is urgently needed. For example, a dream image is not recognized for the latent psychosis it symbolizes, and no appropriate interventions are made.

In Jungian psychology there is also a particular danger of inflation. We see this when a person marvels excessively at the parallels between archetypal images and the themes of one's own or another person's dreams. One can easily fall into the trap of identifying with unconscious archetypal contents or of encouraging others to do so, leading to a state of over-excitement about the material and an overinvolvement in it. This is another birthplace of Jungian wild analysis.

For those who venture, with the best of intentions but naively, into the deep archetypal levels of the mind, terrors can also overtake them when darkness eventually falls. Jung warned repeatedly of the distinct danger of being overwhelmed and crushed by the frightening things one sees in the unconscious. If we are unprepared or depend on a guide not up to the task, we make ourselves vulnerable. Jung suggests that we may then either collapse or turn tail and retreat in a "regressive restoration of the persona" (CW 7, par. 254 ff).

A further temptation to do wild analysis in the Jungian

mode relates to the prospective aspect of the psyche which Jung emphasized (and which, incidentally, makes his psychology so much more popular and more easily acceptable to many people). Jung was not as interested in the repressed contents of the unconscious as he was in those contents which were attempting to break through to an immature ego-consciousness. Compensatory dreams, fantasies and symptoms arise in order to be admitted to the consciousness of an otherwise one-sided personality. The presence of the anima and animus in dreams serves this same function, as do images of the self and other indicators of approaching wholeness. Even shadow problems, though far less attractive and inviting aspects of the personality, are seen to be enhancers of our wholeness once they are acknowledged and integrated.

Jung's psychological insights, as much as Freud's, lend themselves to trivialization and oversimplification. This usually happens when Jung's basic concepts, such as shadow, animus/anima, or the subjective level of dream interpretation are treated in a superficial way. It is true that all elements of a dream may have metaphorical significance or that subpersonality elements may be symbolized as an inner child, as an inner mother or as an inner gorilla for that matter. Jungian wild analysis emerges, however, when a fascination for such psychological material becomes disconnected from a sober and inclusive vision of an individual in his/her personal, clinical and cultural entirety. Fascination with archetypal material without proper grounding leads to some remarkable forms of inflated stupidity.

As meaningful as any of these archetypal images may be, it is very tempting to interpret and apply them to a psyche not at all prepared to deal with them. Too easily we forget Jung's warnings on the mercurial and trickster aspect of the psyche which invites wild analysis as a trap for the foolish. Individuals in Freudian analysis regularly have oedipal dreams while those in Jungian analysis have great archetypal ones. Whose fool are we being if we unconsciously and therefore wildly seize on the bone of someone's juicy archetypal dream and interpret it to them. Care, modesty and at most, cautious enthusiasm, are the only appropriate attitudes to have when we approach psychological material.

It is fascinating to find the dangers and consequences of wild analysis reflected in the myth of Apollo and Cassandra. Apollo was the great god of the sun. His was the power of light and of sight. As Hillman reminds us, Apollo suggests the power of the analytic, of cerebral insight, of untamed desire to see and to act. Apollo sees Cassandra, an anima figure, and wants to ravish her. But Cassandra resists as the psyche will resist any wild analytical intervention. Rejected by Cassandra, Apollo curses her. She is given the ability to prophesy but no one will believe her. Apollonian consciousness precociously, that is, wildly, applied to the anima/soul causes Cassandra's state. One sees, one speaks, but one is not heard. Like Cassandra's prophecies, wild analytic interpretations are ineffectual or, worse, can cause trouble. Both Apollo and Cassandra symbolize the qualities of potentially powerful insight into the tender human soul. Forced together, however, in such a wild fashion, the result is only violation and resistance.

I wish to emphasize that not only do the inflated or the uninitiated constellate and enact the Cassandran fate of "seeing" but of not being heard. Cassandra's fate is also the shadow of every analyst. Freud's psychoanalysis and Jung's analytical psychology bestow an Apollonian power upon the analyst of both insight and understanding. But by looking upon the soul with only Apollonian eyes the analyst will inevitably experience and suffer the fate of Cassandra. The temptation to do wild analysis is really the temptation to force knowledge upon someone not currently able to receive it. Like the knife of the surgeon, which goes directly into the body to repair or remove a problem, a wild interpretation attempts the same thing. But people with psychological knowledge are not like surgeons with their physical knowledge. Neither the professional nor the lay person with psychological knowledge can avoid the fate of Cassandra. We cannot speak the truth about certain psychological matters and expect always to be understood or appreciated. Even if a person, any person, is appropriately cautious and respectful in the attempt to offer a well-timed and gentle interpretation to another, the fate of Cassandra can always infuse itself into the situation and cause difficulties.

Let us hope the practitioner experienced and trained in these matters, in the way Jung had in mind, remains deeply impressed with the power analytic insight gives as well as with the limitations of this power. The Apollonian urge to interpret with single-minded bluntness and to use the muscle of naked insight must be resisted. Cassandra must be our friend as we share her fate. The analyst must listen and observe meditatively with strong Apollonian eyes, but say nothing for long periods of time. For if we speak, we will not be heard. For if we speak, dangerous things may happen. Sometimes what we see may be very subtle and negative, even potentially destructive. Jung described such a situation in his memoir *Memories, Dreams, Reflections*. A man who had come to him for analysis recounted a dream in which Jung saw signs of a latent psychosis. Jung sent the person on his way, saying quite correctly, that he did not need analysis.

The temptation to wild analysis, as Jung has shown us, originates in the psyche itself. One aspect of the psyche, an Apollonian one, feels seduced by and wishes to penetrate into another aspect. This constellation can occur in one degree or another any time an analysis is begun. At this time, the tension of the analyst's Cassandran fate must be acknowledged and contained. We can see, but if we speak, our prophecies will not be heard.

The title of John Kerr's book on the origins of psychoanalysis, *A Most Dangerous Profession* (1993), is appropriate to what I have been describing. The founders of psychoanalysis encountered dangers in their discoveries of how the psyche works and manifests itself. They learned the price that would be paid for acting too quickly in the first flush of these discoveries. Freud, Jung and the other pioneers of psychoanalysis made mistakes, some dreadful ones, as all pioneers must do. We can learn from these mistakes by heeding the warnings they gave us about the dangers of wild analysis. These warnings are particularly pertinent today at a time when so many people crave the quick fix for themselves or for others close to them. Apollonian knowledge is cheap and easily had. Self-help books are convincingly written and marketed widely. But they may only encourage us to repress the fact that things are hard in reality. The psyche does not submit willingly to our Apollonian wishes to correct its problems with the force of an inappropriate psychological interpretation, as "correct" as it may be.

In the final (non-wild) analysis, Apollo and Cassandra must remain in tension. Each reflects a reality which must coexist and interact with the other. When this tension is maintained, a Sophia-like wisdom may emerge which provides a genuine synthesis of these opposites. Here a strong, accurate, and insightful Apollonian knowing is chastened by the Cassandran dilemma, by the limitations of what can be understood or believed by a person. Our Apollonian knowledge cannot be believed until it has stood long enough with Cassandra and been thoroughly chastened by her fate. Then we can understand, either as professional analysts or as ordinary persons wishing to impart psychological insights to others, that Apollonian knowledge cannot be assimilated until it has united with a wisdom which is able to work patiently and slowly with someone's hard realities. This is a wisdom born of the Apollo-Cassandra tension, able to wait for the moment when finally a person's mind is ready to conceive the life of a new insight.

Contributors

MARITA DIGNEY, D.MIN., is a graduate of the C. G. Jung Institute of Zürich and practices in Philadelphia, Pa. She is president of the C. G. Jung Center of Philadelphia.

JAMES HOLLIS, PH.D., is a graduate of the C. G. Jung Institute-Zürich and practices in Philadelphia, Pa. and Linwood, N.J. He is the Director of Education of the C. G. Jung Institute of Philadelphia.

ALDEN JOSEY, PH.D., is a graduate of the C. G. Jung Institute of Zürich and practices in Wilmington, Del.

STEPHEN A. MARTIN, PSY.D., is a graduate of the C. G. Jung Institute of Zürich and practices in Ardmore, Pa. He is president of the Philadelphia Association of Jungian Analysts.

ALEXANDER MCCURDY III, PH.D., is a graduate of the C. G. Jung Institute of Berlin and practices in Radnor, Pa.

POLLY YOUNG-EISENDRATH, PH.D., is a graduate of the Inter-Regional Society of Jungian Analysts and practices in Burlington, Vt., and Philadelphia, Pa. She is a senior research psychologist at the Institute of Pennsylvania Hospital, Philadelphia.